'*A Place at the Table* is a transparent, insightful and intimate portrait of hospitality. Miranda's newly discovered manuscript, shaped into a finished form by her daughter Jo, records a written legacy of hospitality as it was written on every page of her life together with her husband Peter, their family and the wider A Rocha community all over the world. Miranda was luminous with God's light. This book reflects her light and it is a joy to see it on these pages, over and again.'

Sandra McCracken
Singer and songwriter

'I endorse this book as one who has been treated to Miranda's practice of hospitality. The lasting memory of fellowship over a meal in the garden of the Harris home will always live with me . . . The lifelong practice of hospitality shared here is authentic, of lasting impact and worthy of emulation.'

Florence Muindi
Founder, President and CEO of Life in Abundance
International

'The ideal book offers a compelling message that is vital at this cultural moment; it is crafted in a way that is in step with the content and is authored by someone who embodies the subject. This book reveals how hospitality diminishes relational fragmentation and it is written in such a way that feels as if you are around the table. The meal is made complete when you realise that the hosts are a mother and daughter who have lived as exemplars of generosity.'

Rod Wilson
Author, psychologist, President of Regent College,
Vancouver 2000–2015

'Beautifully written, thought provoking and at times poignant, this book weaves together one family's story of love and rootedness with the wisdom born of experience. Jo Swinney draws on biblical insights, practical examples from her own life and the writings of her mother Miranda Harris to explore how giving and receiving hospitality is at the heart of Christian faith.'

Canon Dr Hilary Marlow
Girton College, Cambridge

'This is an emotionally rich and inspiring blend of reflection, story and journal.'

Church Times

A PLACE AT THE TABLE

Faith, hope and hospitality

Miranda Harris and Jo Swinney

HODDER

First published in Great Britain in 2022 by Hodder & Stoughton
An Hachette UK Company

This paperback edition published in 2023

1

A CIP catalogue record for this title is available from the British Library

Paperback ISBN 978 1 529 39206 7
ebook ISBN 978 1 529 39207 4

Typeset in Minion Pro and Futura PT by Hewer Text UK Ltd, Edinburgh
Printed and bound in Great Britain by Clays Ltd, Elcograf S.p.A.

Hodder & Stoughton policy is to use papers that are natural, renewable
and recyclable products and made from wood grown in sustainable
forests. The logging and manufacturing processes are expected to
conform to the environmental regulations of the country of origin.

Hodder & Stoughton Ltd
Carmelite House
50 Victoria Embankment
London EC4Y 0DZ

www.hodderfaith.com

CONTENTS

A NOTE ON THE COVER

The cover art was designed by Karen Sawrey, and depicts *Cruzinha*, the first A Rocha field study centre. The bird at the top left is a hoopoe, which featured on A Rocha's original logo. The colours are taken from a Porches Pottery bowl which Miranda often had sitting on her kitchen table. The unusual perspective is inspired by an icon, *The Trinity* by Andrei Rublev, where the vanishing point is behind the viewer, drawing us into the picture – inviting us to take a place at the table.

FOREWORD

In 2019 Miranda Harris died in a terrible accident in South Africa. Gone, suddenly and unexpectedly, was a woman who had given loving hospitality and a welcoming home to people from all over the world, and to our whole family – granddaughters included. Over the years, my husband and I have welcomed many into our home – even given talks on hospitality. But Miranda lived hospitality with a loving light of warmth in her eyes, which encompassed all who met her.

In 1996 Peter and Miranda Harris came to Regent College – a graduate school of Christian studies in Vancouver, Canada – for a much-needed sabbatical from their twelve years in Portugal. In those years, they and their children had founded and nurtured A Rocha (the Rock), a community that saw the care of creation as central to Christian ministry. Jo Harris, one of those children, tells the story of that twelve-year adventure.

My husband and I, as faculty at Regent College, were eagerly looking forward to learning from the Harris's experience. We were then very disappointed when we realised that we were going to be on sabbatical in Scotland during the whole time they were at Regent. The best we could make of the situation was to invite them to stay in our home on Galiano Island while we were away – which they did.

So we first met Peter and Miranda as they walked down the Galiano Island ferry ramp, pulling their suitcases. They had just arrived; we were about ready to leave. That meeting foreshadowed the many intense, wonderful, but all-too-brief meetings we have had since then. Usually those meetings took place when we or they were departing.

After that first stay on Galiano Island they moved to France to begin another A Rocha community. Several years later they invited us to stay in their home while they came again to our house on Galiano. A few years later they moved to England (to help guide what by now had become an international organisation) – but once again came to Regent, and invited us to stay at their house in England. So we've spent many months in each others' homes: guests in the absence of the host. Something of the beauty and fragility of their life has, we think, soaked into us from the very walls of those homes.

This book, at heart, is a tribute to Miranda, by her eldest daughter Jo. People all over the world have loved and admired Miranda Harris as an exemplar of hospitality. In the twenty-five years of our friendship I have often put her on a lofty pedestal. But neither Jo's loving account of her mother, nor Miranda's notes, allow us to put her on that pedestal of perfection.

We think of hospitality as a welcoming meal – making a place at our table for visitors. This book redefines our understanding of hospitality: the place at the table transmutes to a welcome for others both into, and in spite of, our own messy, exhausted lives. We learn that a welcoming meal can be a nine-course dinner, or simply coffee shared with strangers on a train, or perhaps flowers in the bedroom for a guest. The folks welcomed to the table include not only old friends whom we love to spend time with over a meal, but also unannounced groups of students and needy high-maintenance individuals. All are given the gift of being listened to and welcomed with love.

A Place at the Table could have been yet another of the many hospitality books that make me feel bad about the 'who I am' that falls far short of the 'who I want to be' – and consequently leave me in despair. But this book shows both sides of a coin that gives great wealth to us. On one side of that coin we see the multitude of big and tiny ways to practise giving a place at the table – and on the other side we see the costs: the hard work, the struggle to keep going, the weariness of feeling overwhelmed. Often, when we are tired out from offering hospitality, it is all too easy to be tempted to feel self-pity or even resentment.

We read in the book of Hebrews that Jesus himself was tempted and suffered. We may think, *Well, he didn't really get tempted the way we do*. But the writer of Hebrews emphasises that Jesus was tempted *in every way* just as we are. If we read the Gospels carefully, we see Jesus as the real human being that he was – actively hospitable, whether feeding 5,000 or cooking breakfast on the beach for tired fishermen. But we need to remember that even Jesus needed time alone for rest and prayer. Maybe he was tempted to resent how often those times were interrupted.

Hospitality is not a gift that some people have and some don't; it is a command that is often hard to follow. Again and again in the stories of this book we see the pain and struggles, the problems of fatigue, marital tension and personal sacrifice that have been part of the hospitality of both Miranda and Jo. Jo's insightful retellings of stories from the Bible help us see the realities of hospitality in daily life. All the stories in these pages open our eyes to both the outside and inside joys and jeopardies of practising hospitality. Miranda and Jo make places in their lives to offer a table of nourishing love for others. But this comes with a cost. In opening our lives to others we often have to make hard and seemingly selfish choices. As Edith Shaeffer puts it, in her book *What is a Family*, the door of hospitality needs both 'a hinge and a lock'. Though the doors of A Rocha admitted many guests, Jo describes the eventual need to install a second-floor door to protect the privacy of the family.

The creative touches and loving care in the hospitality of both Jo and Miranda are wonderful; we see a broad scope of ways to welcome and love. Yet a greater gift is their honesty, their willingness to show their dark side and human struggles, their willingness to be vulnerable to our inveterate judgement. They don't let us put them on pedestals. Instead they show us the only solid foundation for hospitality: the Rock (A Rocha) of our faith in a God of love.

So let me tell you about some of the lessons in hospitality given to me by Miranda. Years ago Miranda shared the acronym DMC, her term for Deeply Meaningful Conversations. For both of us, just getting from the door into Regent College, up a wide staircase to the door of our office inevitably involved many 'hello's that evolved into heart-to-heart conversations – the DMCs. Miranda's willingness to share that, for her, DMCs were both deeply good and deeply draining was healing for me: she was human, I was human; it was okay and not some sinful lack of caring to flop with fatigue after DMCs.

Once when we were with Peter and Miranda in their home after another house trade, I admired a beautiful little Provence-patterned pot for *herbes d'Provence*. She insisted that I take it. In doing so I learned a lesson: giving and receiving cherished things can bring great joy.

Another time was a DMC between Miranda and me as we sat on the back of a truck at the Brooksdale A Rocha Canada Centre. We laughed and discussed thoughts and concerns with freedom and trust. We shared weaknesses and confessed that sometimes a glass of wine gives gladness amid busyness. We didn't talk about any strong undercurrent of grace; but it was for sure there in our God-with-us DMC.

In these pages Miranda and Jo offer us a place at the table of their lives. That place gives us spiritual and emotional wealth, precisely because we see both the glory in the abundance found at their table, and the cost involved in preparing that place for others. In his letter to the Corinthians, Paul discusses God's response to the weakness that tormented him: 'My grace is sufficient for you, for my power is made perfect in weakness' (2 Cor. 12:9). Their willingness to be vulnerable in admitting weakness is a gift for all of us. In Christ, and the place he gives to us at *his* table of bread and wine, we join with Paul, and Jo and Miranda, as we, in and through our weakness, offer a place at the table to all the others whom Christ brings into our lives.

Mary-Ruth Wilkinson
Sessional Lecturer at Regent College, Vancouver, Canada
March 2022

PROLOGUE

Let's begin with a bold idea. Might hospitality be as close to the heart of a lived Christian faith as churchgoing, financial giving or Bible reading? There is something irrefutably uncompromising in these words from Paul to the young church in Rome, as direct as any of his exhortations and as clear: 'Be joyful in hope, patient in affliction, faithful in prayer. Share with the Lord's people who are in need. Practise hospitality' (Rom. 12:12–13).

But while hospitality was woven into the cultural fabric of his first-century Mediterranean audience and remains so in much of the Global South, for many of us in materially comfortable, individualistic twenty-first-century settings, it is a lost art. It is a practice we have forgotten, neglected or distorted beyond all recognition, so some reassurance might be welcome. To be hospitable, you do not need to know how to make squares of fabric into elaborate shapes. You do not need to have mastered French, Italian, Indian or indeed any country's cuisine. You do not need to have unchipped glasses and matching plates, silver cutlery and specific knives for fish, butter and cheese. You do not need to have a stock of witty anecdotes or a dust-free home.

You can, in fact, be hospitable without a home. Among the classiest hospitality I have ever received was in an ancient campervan in Italy. I have also shared a packed lunch with a neighbouring car in log-jammed traffic, been offered coffee in a bus shelter and been wrapped in the tenderest care by a homeless teen as I cried under a tree in a city park. Hospitality at its heart is just that: the offer of kindness and care and a place to belong for a while. We can all do that, even if it is something we aren't naturally inclined towards. As we give and receive hospitality of different kinds, in a variety of contexts, we mirror the heart of God, who desires us to share our lives with him. Jesus spoke of the home he has waiting for us, and also of his hope that we will open the door to him, so he can sit at *our* table: 'Here I am! I stand at the door and knock. If anyone hears my voice and opens the door, I will come in and eat with that person, and they with me' (Rev. 3:20).

There are twin hopes for the words in this book. The first is that they will help you towards a deeper understanding of the hospitality God offers us all. His love really can satisfy the gnawing hunger and raging thirst of our souls. There is always a place at his table for you. The second hope is that you will be encouraged to make hospitality a more routine part of your life. That the pot on your stove will always be full enough to feed an extra mouth. That your schedule will have flexibility for an unplanned coffee and a chat. That your door will be often open and that, in all these small acts of welcome, you will see God at work, knitting you into closer, deeper and more life-giving relationships than you could have dreamed possible.

This is a book about food and friendship, community and belonging, the table, the earth and the sea. Much of what you will read is grounded in the story of an organisation. In September

1983, a small seed was planted and began to grow in the dry, sandy soil of the Algarve in Southern Portugal. This seed, A Rocha, withstood drought and pests, taking root and growing strong. Today it bears fruit on six continents. Its presence can be seen from space, and many are the landscapes that flourish because it grows there.

A Rocha, meaning 'the rock' in Portuguese, is a worldwide family of organisations working in nature conservation in obedience to and worship of the Creator. In the early 1980s, scientists had begun to sound an alarm. It was all but ignored by Christians, to the point that the concept of a Christian charity with an environmental focus frequently provoked laughter, if not ire: why waste time on birds when there are souls to save? A few short decades later and only someone with a twisted sense of humour would laugh at the disaster unfolding before our eyes. We have treated God's world with breathtaking contempt, over-consuming, pouring toxic waste into our rivers and lakes, filling our oceans with plastic and our air with carbon dioxide, wiping out entire species without a second's consideration, grief or guilt – all this while some of us say we love the one who made it, sustains it and has imbued it with his glory. In the dining room at Cruzinha, the first of A Rocha's field study centres, there is a painted tile plaque displaying Psalm 24:1: 'The earth is the LORD's, and everything in it.' This is why the care of creation is a Christian concern – his concerns are ours.

I am the eldest daughter of A Rocha's founders, Peter and Miranda Harris, and now its director of communications. It is my job to tell our stories, of which one of my favourites is the time Mum, given an impossibly small budget to furnish Cruzinha, blew most of it on a 100-year-old handmade wooden table. It became the heart of the house and around it, disparate humans came together to eat, talk and become family. In Leah Kostamo's book, *Planted*, which tells the story of A Rocha Canada, she writes, 'At A Rocha centres we don't have a chapel, we have a

3

table. The meal is a place of community, fellowship and invitation . . . the table is a safe place, a neutral ground for dialogue, knowing and communion.'[1]

As A Rocha has grown, we have held on to our commitment to closely lived interpersonal relationships as the context for our work of science, conservation and environmental education. Not all of our organisations have residential centres like that first one in Portugal where I grew up, but all prioritise communal life, and communal life means eating together.

After our family left Portugal in 1995 when I was seventeen, my story diverged from A Rocha's. I followed the twists and turns with great interest, but from a distance. For me, growing up meant not only differentiating from my parents, as all of us must, but from an organisation that in some ways had raised me too. After leaving high school, I travelled, studied, met and married Shawn and had two daughters, Alexa and Charis. I worked, first, for an epilepsy charity and then as a freelance writer and editor, and then in a couple of communications roles. And then something happened that pulled me back into A Rocha's orbit in a way I could never have foreseen.

On 29 October 2019, Shawn, the girls and I were heading for a few days away in a rented cottage when Shawn's phone rang. My uncle's voice sounded strained, and he asked Shawn to pull over and call him back. We stopped at the top of a hill, England's gentle greens and greys laid out before us, all but invisible to me as my mind raced through possible scenarios. Shawn walked down the slope out of earshot and, when the call finally ended, he came back towards me with red eyes. He said we needed to return home. Once there, he'd tell me what had happened. He was so sorry, he said, but it was a very hard thing he'd have to say.

Knowing the girls were watching us, I was calm, though I remember I struggled to figure out how to open the car door. The girls were full of anxious questions, and I told them that whatever happened we would be okay because God was good, and he loved us. Then we drove the short distance home in silence.

We have a genetic condition in our family which has given my dad some close shaves. If I had any thought on that drive, it was to brace myself for the news that something had happened to him. What Shawn had to tell me, and later my three siblings, was that both my parents, along with A Rocha International's executive director Chris Naylor and his wife Susanna and their driver, had been in a road accident in Port Elizabeth, South Africa, where they had been for work. And the Naylors and Mum had been killed.

Death may be a certainty but, whenever and however it comes, it is shocking. A person was there, and then, though their body remains for a while, they are gone. How can this be? I think we know in our bones that we were made for permanence, which makes death an outrage, an offence, all but impossible to grasp. All the images and allusions to heaven in the Bible point to future bodies made to last, but until resurrection day we can be mortally wounded. We can find ourselves one minute mid-conversation, barrelling along an ocean-side highway towards the airport and home. The next, after a split second of chaos and noise – time's up. According to medical examiners, before the vehicle had finished its hellish descent from bridge to concrete embankment to water, three lives had ended and only two remained.

The next few days are a blur. The best way I can describe how it felt is to compare it to active labour: intervals of all-consuming pain followed by interludes of welcome numbness during which decisions had to be made, actions taken, conversations held. The endlessly patient consultant overseeing Dad's care used the words 'critical but stable' and urged us to come. So the four of us siblings found ourselves together in South Africa, gathered around his bed.

Jesus made those of us who follow him into a family. His family did him proud during those weeks in South Africa. Christian friends put us up at no cost in a suite in their hotel. The church in

Port Elizabeth mobilised, and nourishing meals arrived at the door at regular intervals. On the night following the small cremation service, we sat around a local pastor's firepit eating steaks and watching the stars, wrapped in blankets and the kindness of strangers. Back at home, my friend messaged to say she'd been part of a protection detail doing its best to hold off a bombardment of lasagnes coming at the house. Lasagne is the love language of our church.

When we first arrived, Dad was ventilated, in an induced coma. He had two punctured lungs, fourteen fractured ribs, a broken sternum and right shoulder and a bruised heart. He had tubes and monitors everywhere and he was almost unrecognisable. The vehicle had landed upside down, his heart had stopped, and his head was underwater when rescuers pulled him out. Had an experienced lifesaver not been on the bridge and made it to his side within a two-minute window, he would have died. It could be categorised as a case of the right person in the right place at the right time: a fortunate coincidence, if you will. But there is no category other than 'miracle' for the fact that the medical condition I mentioned earlier didn't kill him. There's an awkwardness to that solitary miracle when three more were needed. Another mystery to leave in the hands of God, whose wisdom no one can fathom.

Let's move forward in time, past the milestones of Dad's physical recovery, the return to England, Mum's funeral, the first Christmas and bleak winter months of debilitating grief and painstaking graft of carving a new life without this vivid, beautiful, loving woman. Let's acknowledge in passing the new life imposed on us all by a global pandemic, when we isolated and distanced and grew wary of each other and soon discovered you could be as hungry for company as for food. And let's pause for a moment, on a grey day in February 2021.

The time had come for Dad to take another brave step and leave the house he and Mum had called home for ten years. It was too big for one, and too far from close family and friends. We had been slowly sorting for months, and on this particular day we decided to tackle Mum's study. It wasn't a big room and it looked tidy and ordered. There was a chest of drawers, a bookshelf, a desk and a small sofa, and a window that looked out over the back garden and the Wiltshire countryside beyond. As we worked, a pile grew in the middle of the room, a mountain of paper covered in her distinctive handwriting. There were talk notes, drafts of articles, newsletters, journals and jottings. And then I found a blue ring-binder that momentarily winded me.

Mum had talked about writing a book for more than twenty years. Many of us had cheered her on in this endeavour, knowing her gift with words, her ability to perceive and capture life as she lived it, and the depth and breadth of experience from which she could draw. But as time went by, I confess I lost faith she'd produce the goods. I wept as I looked through this binder, evidence of her labour and the distillation of what she wanted to say to the world. What I held in my hands was not a full manuscript, but it was enough, alongside the many other words she had poured onto other pages, to become the basis of what you now hold in your hands.

I don't know when she wrote these next words, but they were written for now and they belong here.

This book has been a LONG time in gestation. I talked over the ideas with John Stott and Eugene Peterson well over a decade ago and both were encouraging and interested. In the intervening years I have worked on the manuscript with my husband, daughter and sister, each time simultaneously dealing with genuine excitement and pangs of remorse that my yearning to write had once more been shelved.

I have always written and always loved writing. For many years I have been aware of a book inside me, present and growing, sometimes sleeping and occasionally delivering an impatient kick. Time after time, when I came close to abandoning the project, someone (and sometimes three or four people in a week) would say, 'You *must* write.' And I would keep going.

There have been a number of contributors to my procrastination, but I haven't ever been able to entirely ignore or lay down this book. You can only ignore fire in your bones for so long before you get burnt.

I can imagine John Stott and Eugene Peterson hosting the most amazing launch party for Mum in heaven, the angels rejoicing with her at the long-awaited birth of this book, Jesus glowing with pride and delight in his daughter Miranda, the author.

This is a book we have written together, she and I. You will know when she's speaking, and you will know when it is me. She wrote in a letter to a friend in a tough situation that the darkest places are often the most fertile: the womb, the soil, the deepest parts of the ocean. This book has been birthed in the darkness of her absence, but in its pages you will get to meet her and, in some mysterious way, maybe even experience her hospitality.

On one of the pieces of scrap paper in her study she had written that once she was 'fretting about the meaning of my existence and what I had to offer as I lived and worked among a collection of very gifted people. My sister, who is a woman of prayer and discernment, said very simply, "You were born to love people." This has been a hugely liberating insight. What an honour! I'm so glad my gift didn't turn out to be writing mathematics textbooks or addressing theology students in Ancient Greek.'

To know Miranda was to know the truth of my aunt's words. She had a rare capacity for love and myriad ways to show it. Throughout her adult years, she grew in her commitment to the practice of hospitality and, more specifically, cooking for people, and gave deep and careful thought to its significance. Most of all, she knew it as a tangible expression of her love and, through her, God's love.

The meal is an opportunity for connection. It involves growing or shopping for the ingredients, trying to make choices that honour the Earth and its people, blessing not exploiting them; it involves God's gift of time and place. The preparation, setting, serving at the table and clearing up all involve handling creation, being part of it, relationship with it.

Growing takes time, whether it is relationships or vegetables. That's why it's important to look into each other's eyes and to eat together – to plant, grow, harvest, prepare, celebrate and clean up together.

Hospitality is not about parading your perfect home, culinary magic or immaculate children before your admiring (and demoralised) guests. Rather it is inviting other hassled people to come and eat, talk and laugh with you over the idiosyncrasies and impossibilities of your lives in the secure, cosy environment of your own intractable mess. If I exaggerate, I do so only slightly. As Philip Yancey wrote, 'In the presence of the Great Physician my most appropriate contribution may be my wounds.'[2]

We are not called by God to impress others; we are called to bless them. People are immensely encouraged by our failures and flaws. A great way to build community is to acknowledge our limitations, step aside and give others the chance to shine. Opening our homes and our lives as they are is a way of loving others and creating conditions for communion. If we offer people our real selves, we give them permission to be real too.

If you were one of the multitudes who spent time at Mum's table, you will know she would have given careful thought to what to serve you. She would have gone to Robert Douse, the local butcher, for the meat, where she'd have stayed for a while to catch up on how his family were doing and probably tell him all about you and what she was going to serve you for dinner. She'd have found organic vegetables and, if eggs were on the menu, they'd have come from the house up the lane near her home.

As she cooked, she'd have listened to music and quite possibly danced around the kitchen, and she would have been praying intermittently. She was the most prayerful person I have ever known. Now and then she would have paused to enjoy a particularly glossy tulip in the vase on the windowsill, the photos of friends tacked over the cupboards or a handmade card from one of the grandchildren. She would have set the table with great care and always with candles in the centre. As your arrival drew near, she might have become a little flustered and stressed over last-minute timings. She was human, after all. But the moment you were there, you would be her entire focus. 'Come in!' she'd say, radiant in welcome. 'It is so good to have you here.' And you would step into the fragrant smells of her cooking and the warmth of her embrace and know you were about to enjoy a wonderful evening around her table.

My prayer is that, as you spend time with her and with me through our words, you will keep having to leave us to pop an invitation to lunch through your neighbour's door, or to stir the soup, or to add something to your grocery list. May you listen to the Holy Spirit's whispered reminder that you have a forever home in your Father's house and smile as you set about echoing his welcome to someone who needs it.

A NOTE ON THE CONTENTS

There are many kinds of writing in this book and so lots of ways you might want to read it other than the standard beginning-to-end approach (which is fine too).

The book is structured around the progression of a meal, from its planning to the moment every guest has departed and every pan has been cleaned, or is at least soaking in the sink. Every chapter begins with some general discussion of the theme at hand. I drew my mum's writing here from a variety of places. Some of it she had written for her planned book about community and belonging. I have also used transcripts and notes of talks she gave, excerpts of articles, blogs and pieces of the newsletters she sent and diligently filed away in chronological order. To maintain the flow, I have not noted where each specific part came from. The typography will show you whether it is me or Mum speaking at any given time.

Then there are Bible stories, each of which I have retold from the perspective of an imagined participant. Mum loved the Bible. She found time to read it most days, even while travelling and during the very fullest years of parenting and leading A Rocha. She'd include carefully chosen passages in her letters and cards and prayed the Psalms year in and year out with Dad each morning. I love the Bible too and believe it is inspired by the Spirit to reveal the character and intentions of God.

The Bible is full of accounts of meals, from the Israelites' snatched repast of lamb and flatbread the night before their escape from Egypt, to the dull-but-lifesaving daily dinners of manna and quail in the desert years, to Daniel and his friends' plain vegetarian fare in Babylon, and all the many times recounted in the Gospels when Jesus enjoyed good food and conversation. Rather than drawing out worthy lessons, I wanted to help you engage imaginatively with some of these occasions, pulling you inside the story to see and feel their impact and significance for yourself. I have done the background work to make these pieces as faithful to the time and text as possible while allowing myself a bit of creative licence here and there. If you go back to the Bible to check on the details, you might be surprised at how vivid and observant the original writing actually is. I found there was generally a lot to work with.

The final component is a selection of Mum's journal entries dating from 1983 to 2019. These are interspersed between each chapter and are not linked to the chapter themes. You may get engrossed and decide to read the journals from beginning to end without interruption – that is probably what I would do. The journals tell the story of how A Rocha grew around the practice of hospitality and the part it played in our family life.

Most of this writing was new to me, discovered as I pulled together material for the book. It has given me a deeper understanding of what it was like for Mum to pioneer an innovative mission organisation in a variety of foreign cultures on a shoestring. Her faith, humour and enormous capacity for relationship are woven through every entry, as are her struggles with shaky self-confidence, exhaustion and the endless goodbyes – the sting in the tail of all those hellos. She believed in the power of vulnerability; her willingness to live 'inside out' was itself an act of generous and sacrificial hospitality, allowing others to really know her and, in turn, be known.

So, there you go – a smorgasbord! Bon appétit.

ONE

HUNGER

Hunger finds no fault with the cook.

C. H. SPURGEON

The feeling of hunger is not pleasant. It causes growly, volcanic activity in the stomach, headaches, irritability and dizziness. It can make concentration hard, as thoughts of food become increasingly intrusive. If hunger were a person, they would be a sharp-elbowed nagging harridan, getting more obnoxiously bossy the longer they were ignored.

In places where food is affordable and abundant, we can avoid hunger, grazing a path between meals without so much as a murmured grumble from our sated stomachs. But is it actually a

13

good idea to do that? Might there be losses as well as gains to this approach?

All truly great meals begin with hunger. If you have ever been on a long hike, sustained only by a packet of peanuts and a bottle of water, I'm guessing you would have awarded a Michelin star to whatever landed on your plate that night. Food tastes exponentially better to the hungry; as Proverbs 27:7 puts it:

One who is full loathes honey from the comb,
but to the hungry even what is bitter tastes sweet.

We may not enjoy the sensation, but hunger is a God-given gift, an inbuilt reminder to seek out what we need to live and to experience joy in doing so.

I love cooking for people, and for several years gladly took on the task of feeding a church group that met in our home once a fortnight to study the Bible. It was largely made up of students and overworked young professionals who would show up straight from the train out of London. I took it as a great compliment when, after a few weeks, one of the group, Alex, announced on the doorstep that he had not eaten all day in order to be able to stuff himself with what he expected to be a very tasty meal. Unfortunately, on that occasion I had run out of time and Shawn had persuaded me that everyone would be just as happy with frozen pizza. Perhaps Alex was hungry enough to transform the cardboardy base and greasy cheese into a gourmet delight but, for me, it was a missed opportunity to enjoy watching someone dive in up to their eyeballs in a casserole of my making.

When you have put time, care and money into creating a feast, you want hungry people around the table. A ravenous diner is visibly relieved of physical and mental discomfort, fork by forkful, relaxing into the experience and gradually tuning in to the details of flavour and texture, colour and composition. You have soothed, nurtured and delighted. Your work has not been in vain.

On the contrary, if someone has eaten shortly before they arrived and have no need or desire for what you serve up, you'd be forgiven for feeling rather insulted, if not hurt. Do they not trust your cooking? Do they not care about your feelings? Well might you ask. But there are many reasons why people avoid hunger, so we don't necessarily have to take it personally.

The primary purpose of food may be to sustain life, but it can be used effectively as a way of soothing away dark feelings or boredom. There is a real possibility that a person turning up for a meal at someone's house might be anxious about the occasion. Perhaps they are shy or depressed, or have some kind of tricky history with a fellow invitee that you don't know about. And they may have indulged in what is known as 'comfort eating' as a coping mechanism.

After school I spent a year in Dijon, France, working as a nanny for a family with a toddler and a baby. The initial few months were lonely and isolated and, while my confidence began to grow in the home context, an uncomfortable element began to intrude. Madame was friendly but reserved before I withdrew from them to my room in the evening. However, Monsieur took to giving me a goodnight hug. I was uneasy about this, feeling that some invisible boundary had been breached.

My misgivings multiplied later during a family holiday to the Midi. When we went on an afternoon walk, he got us lost as dusk was falling and felt it would be safer to grab my hand as we fought through the tangled vegetation in what I fervently hoped was the direction of home. On another occasion, for my birthday, I was invited to a concert, but in the event Madame couldn't or didn't come. So again, I found myself caught in the crossfire of questions. Is this an okay situation, or is it, in fact, as weird as it feels? Is this kindness or taking advantage? Would I like a drink afterwards? *Bien sûr, d'accord.* We went to a café, not a bar, but I sipped my hot chocolate warily and was grateful to get back to the sanctuary of my room shortly afterwards. Nothing improper ever happened, but how do you identify appropriate relational boundaries in a foreign context when neither culture nor language are familiar?

Around this time, my weight began to spiral out of control; a combination of unhappiness and boredom conspired to propel me into the warm, fragrant-smelling patisseries instead of past them. As my girth expanded, so my self-esteem shrank. In my free time, armed with my slender earnings, I began to hunt for clothes, less to adorn than to disguise the body I was beginning to dislike. One day I found a pair of olive-green velvet trousers which I knew would transform me into the svelte teenager I believed I really was. 'Do you, er, have the next size up? Um . . . perhaps the one after that?' Tug, squeeze, gasp, then the tears of despair coming down flushed cheeks in the merciless mirror of the changing cubicle.

This is, of course, not rocket science. There is a whole booming industry dedicated to separating people from their money in exchange for promises of personal transformation. As for the patisseries, loneliness has always led to comfort eating and other activities equally or more destructive of a person's self-worth. In my case, as in most, terrible internal conflict raged – my desperate longing to shed kilos advanced against an irresistible desire for quiche and *tarte aux pommes.* Time after time the defeated enemy retreated, weakened and demoralised. Again and again, just one more chunk of still-warm baguette, smothered in butter and dipped in a bowl of steaming *café au lait* promised the necessary consolation. The resulting return of strength and resolve provoked the next onslaught, and the process began once more.

In some cultures, including my own, the prevailing consensus that thin bodies are more attractive and, therefore, of higher value than fat ones has led to mass dysfunctionality around food. The year I spent in Zimbabwe as a nineteen-year-old was a revelation, not only because of the constant proximity to those living without food security but also because my generous posterior was so highly prized I couldn't walk a hundred metres without a proposal of marriage and a chorus of loud appreciation for this previously maligned attribute of mine. For that brief window of time, I glimpsed a world where food was all blessing and my body the ideal shape. And I liked it very much.

In some parts of the world, people are starving; in others, they are spending eye-watering sums of money on low-calorie meal-replacement shakes, pills preventing fat absorption, stomach stapling and wrist bands that buzz angrily if you haven't burnt enough energy. 'Diet culture' has normalised the practice of overriding the body's clear communication about what it needs to be healthy and happy. As someone who belonged to various diet clubs for *an entire decade*, not to mention the years and years prior where I followed restrictive food rules of my own devising, I can tell you (as can the science) that this is the very best way not only to mess up your metabolism but also to build a prison of fear, to bore your friends silly and, the real kicker, ultimately to get fatter for your trouble. Studies have shown that the vast majority of dieters regain all weight lost and usually a bit extra within three years.[1]

One of these diet clubs I went to sold itself on the promise that you could lose weight and NEVER FEEL HUNGRY! To that end, we were encouraged to binge on what the programme termed 'free foods'. Never mind if you didn't like them or felt a certain quantity was probably enough, you should fill up because otherwise hunger would come calling and all hell would break loose. You might start eating things you really like, and then what? Never stop? So, I confess, I was one of those people who got invited to dinner and showed up having just scoffed two hard-boiled eggs, a tin of tuna, six carrots and a tub of that crime against dairy, Quark. All so I wouldn't be tempted to eat and enjoy a reasonable portion of the delicious chicken and bacon pie with buttery mashed potato lovingly served by my kind host.

The Bible says gluttony is a sin so serious that Proverbs 23:2 advises those of us so inclined to put a knife to our throats. Oh dear. Let me tell you, nothing spawns gluttony more effectively than self-inflicted deprivation. During my years and years of dieting, I discovered how exhausting and ineffective it is to rely on your own reserves of self-control. It was like maintaining a leaky dam in a mighty river. Galatians 5:16 says, 'live by the Spirit, and you will not gratify the desires of the flesh'. That is because the Holy Spirit within us produces godly character and good fruit. It is the Spirit who enables us to 'live a life worthy of' our calling (Eph. 4:1), not our own willpower.

Another reason we might avoid hunger is that it reminds us we are fragile, mortal beings, a handful of meals from demise. We do not have all we need to survive within ourselves. Without regular fuel we die, and death – especially our own – is something we try to ignore. But 'a wise person thinks a lot about death' (Eccles. 7:4, NLT). Facing the reality of our dependence on God can only be a good exercise. And we need not fear. This final enemy has, after all, been decisively defeated by Jesus on the cross.

REAL HUNGER

I don't know how long I was on the drip in casualty; I do know that it didn't seem to help the pain much, that the lights were very bright and the young female doctor remote and not at all reassuring. I was stranded for several hours in a white gown on a white table in a white room. And when they sent us home without finding anything wrong, although the July morning was beautiful, the outlook felt very bleak.

Mercifully the family had slept through it all, our son obligingly transferring to the sofa in his half sleep to be closer to the phone. For the next thirty-six hours I lay tossing and turning, being very sick and soaking the pillow with my dripping face. At night I wandered wretchedly around the house looking for a way of sitting or lying that was manageable. Peter was infinitely patient and gentle with me, trying to keep fluids in and simultaneously organising everyone else, including a couple of visitors. Eventually our doctor decided to send us back to hospital, thinking maybe it wasn't gastroenteritis at all, and it was she who hastily arranged everything with Monsieur Becaud, the surgeon, suspecting the intussusception of the small intestine that it turned out to be and knowing all too well the need for prompt action.

On day four after surgery, I entered a world totally dominated by the bathroom as, miraculously, the rudely disrupted internal scenery settled back into a more recognisable landscape. Everyone said how *wonderfully* everything was working again as I made my way yet again to the en suite, accompanied by a wheeled apparatus clanking and rattling like a crazy palm tree with its canopy of inverted bags and bottles. I was safe, albeit sleepless and utterly weak. I was also hungry – very hungry. This was the eighth day without food, and I was experiencing another new sensation: an empty stomach. The night, however, was far from over. There were at least three hours to wait. We are not used to waiting in our culture.

Dawn broke at last in multicoloured loveliness soon after 6.00 a.m. As a three-year-old daughter reminded us once, 'We must be thankful for small mercies!' So I smiled as the junior nurse placed a cup of weak tea and two dry biscuits on my tray, disguising my disappointment with an insincere attempt at gratitude. A bowl of thin, lukewarm soup arrived at lunch-time. There must be something else on the menu – steak and chips, for example?

Food began to occupy a larger corner of my mind. 'What are we having this evening?' I asked later, trying to sound casual but fantasising about small pieces of white fish, mashed potato and little florets of bright green broccoli. She lifted the lid. Small curls of pasta with a sprinkling of Gruyère to disguise the blandness sat in the middle of the plate like the pale yolk of a poached egg.

As the days passed, I grew a little ashamed of my temporary obsession with the nice lady who drove the food trolley. Uncomfortable images stored from years of exposure to the media and several journeys to Africa, of wide, empty, pleading eyes and distended bellies belonging to small people with no hope of any trolley appearing over the horizon any time soon, began to impose themselves on my self-absorbed imagination. Unwittingly and unwillingly, I was beginning to identify with many for whom hunger is the norm.

The hunger most of us in the Global North experience has little to do with real need for food – we have enough reserves in our fat and liver cells to carry us through a good many missed meals. Hunger is the *perception* of need and is very much connected to our habits. At the times we are used to eating, our bodies get ready to be fed: glands in our mouths produce saliva, our stomachs fill with digestive juices and our intestines begin to practise contracting. Ironically, at the point of starvation, the desire to eat is long gone. Dr Paul Brand, a doctor who worked for many years in India, wrote about his experiences of treating children with kwashiorkor, where long-term malnutrition has led to severe protein deficiency:

> Hunger no longer drives the child to cry and seek food. As death approaches, apathy has replaced hunger ... Perhaps it is a merciful provision of the Creator that when further effort or fight has become futile, the sense of hunger is alleviated. Death comes gently, like a friend.[2]

Farmers produce enough food to feed the world, yet just under 700 million go to bed hungry every night, largely owing to poverty, conflict and localised impacts of climate change.[3] If we continue to over-consume and use production methods that deplete nutrients in the soil, pollute the water and eradicate the pollinators, hunger will eventually be an acute problem for all of us. But is it now? As a member of a generally very well-fed society, do I have anything to do with those starving in faraway lands? And if I do, how could I possibly make a difference when the need is so acute?

I don't think there is any way of wriggling out of our individual and corporate responsibility for the suffering of others, whether they are around the corner or on a different continent. God's passionate concern for those in need is writ large throughout the Bible and his primary means of helping them is us: his hands and feet on earth. Hungry people are our problem. 'From everyone who has been given much, much will be demanded,' said Jesus (Luke 12:48).

This could all become rather crushing if it wasn't for the fact that God knows better than anyone that no single person can make a dent in a problem as massive as world hunger. But each of us can make some choices: to acknowledge not ignore those who go hungry; to share our resources with the greatest possible impact; to make steps towards a more sustainable diet, reducing our meat consumption and food waste, for example; and to add our voices to others calling for just and wise policies around food production, distribution and sale, until all our voices together make a noise loud enough to demand attention.

We make these choices not only because they may one day be the factor that creates critical mass but also because they are the right choices. Who we are and how we live is determined by a long series of small decisions, not a handful of grand gestures. There may not be a clear right or wrong dichotomy at each moment of decision, but if we are honest and in tune with our conscience and with the still, small voice of the Holy Spirit, we'll admit there is often a more right or a more wrong option, and we don't always go with the former. The more we do the godly thing, whatever the cost, the more we look like Jesus, Light of the World:

If you spend yourselves on behalf of the hungry
and satisfy the needs of the oppressed,
then your light will rise in the darkness,
and your night will become like the noonday.
(Isaiah 58:10)

Jesus has made it our business to care that there are malnourished babies who, if they survive to adulthood, will be stunted and weakened. It is our problem that, even in wealthy nations, there are those who can't afford three meals a day. Once we make our peace with that fact, we can get on and work together to build a table big enough to fit the whole family around.

STARVING FOR COMPANY

Hospitality is not just about food. Sometimes what people *really* need (and, hard though it is to believe, more than cake) is human connection. Public health studies have found links between loneliness and heart disease, stroke, dementia and poor immune function. It turns out feeling isolated and disconnected is really very bad for you, bad enough to shorten your lifespan significantly.[4]

During my last two years at school, my friend Claudia and I went to visit an elderly lady called Mrs Green one afternoon a week as part of a volunteer scheme. Before we rang her doorbell, we would have to psych ourselves up to the ordeal of breathing the stale, over-boiled-cabbage-scented air in her ground-floor flat. The fresh air we brought in with us was the only fresh air to enter the hermetically sealed dwelling week by week. Mrs Green had found herself in her mid-eighties entirely alone in the world. This 'pair of silly girls', as she called us, was all she had.

Each week, we'd arrive just as she was about to tuck into a hearty high tea of sandwiches and tasty-looking confectionery, and we'd sit watching hungrily as she ate it all up. Never once did she offer us so much as a glass of water. After this uncomfortable ritual, she'd say, 'You haven't dusted my lightbulbs in months, girls.' And we'd fetch the feather duster and perform this important task, before watching snooker on her black and white TV until it was time to go. We began telling tall tales to keep things interesting. Claudia met a boy on holiday in Greece, became engaged and planned to elope, all of which Mrs Green greeted with sensible incredulity, even when we brought in a ring as 'proof'.

Eventually we wore her down with our constant questioning, and she told us parts of her life story. Mrs Green had been a kept woman, living all expenses paid as the long-term mistress of a man called Tom. Then one day she'd gone on holiday to Africa (country unknown) to be met at the airport on her return by her brother, who called out over the barrier at Arrivals, 'Tom's dead!' She went to the funeral and caused a scene, and that was that. As far as we could gather, she had no family and no friends and saw no one regularly, other than the two of us.

Mrs Green was interminably pessimistic, and as we'd cheerily wave goodbye and say, 'See you next week!' she'd reply in her broad Gloucestershire accent, 'That's if I'm still alive . . .' This always set us off in peals of giggles, callous youths that we were. I like to think she grew fond of us, though, despite all evidence to the contrary. We certainly grew fond of her.

In 2018, the UK appointed a Minister for Loneliness to help nine million citizens who often or always feel lonely.[5] That same year, in a survey of twenty thousand Americans, almost half said they did not have meaningful in-person social interactions on a daily basis. In the 1980s, similar studies found only 20 per cent felt that way.[6] The COVID-19 pandemic will no doubt have exacerbated the trend as, around the world, the many who live alone have been reduced to screen-mediated interactions.

We are at risk of becoming seriously cut off from each other. The very technologies that are designed to facilitate communication can become a barrier to it. If we want to watch a film, we download it instead of going to the cinema with friends. If we can't agree what to watch, we can each choose something different and watch it on our own. If we need to know something, we ask Google. And that nice lady we used to talk to in the bank? She lost her job a long time ago. Basically, everything we need is just a couple of clicks away.

I should say, however, that it's too easy to be cynical about the internet and its erosion of 'real' relationships, as cyberspace has also provided unrivalled arenas for connection, support and social activism.

Whether we meet online or in person, we need connection. In practising hospitality, we can satisfy our own and another's hunger for company, simply through the gift of presence. Undivided attention, quality eye contact, careful non-judgemental listening, shared belly laughter – these are as nourishing as a root vegetable and barley stew with crusty sourdough on a cold winter's night, and as warming. You are seen. You are accepted. You are not alone. How badly we all need to hear these words expressed in an unhurried conversation, an arm around the shoulder, a probing question.

As we can avoid hunger by eating junk food, so we can dull the pain of loneliness by surrounding ourselves with crowds of pseudo-friends. Soap opera characters, Instagram followers, TikTok posters, vocal strangers on special interest Facebook pages or in overcrowded WhatsApp groups can take the place of deep, true relationships. We are able to use these interactions to drown out distress signals designed to avert disaster. But if we allow ourselves to feel the full force of our loneliness, it can drive us out to make or deepen a relationship. God made it so.

SPIRITUAL FOOD

We crave acceptance. We crave love. And we know that if anyone could see inside, they'd be as shocked and disappointed as we are ourselves. Not God, though. As the Dutch pastor and writer Henri Nouwen said in his book, *Life of the Beloved*, we must 'change from living life as a painful test to prove that you deserve to be loved, to living it as an unceasing "Yes" to the truth of that Belovedness'.[7]

Have you ever been told or said to someone else, 'God is all you need'? It sounds like it should be true, but it isn't, not in the literal sense anyway. Consider: man may not live by bread alone, but man does need bread. Adam walked with God in the garden of Eden, but he also needed human company (Gen. 2:18–22). God has clothed us in righteousness, but in public settings we need to be clothed in clothes too, or we risk being arrested for indecent exposure. Spiritual hunger is real, but so too is hunger for food and relationships.

That said, our need for God runs deeper than all other hungers. Even after satisfying every appetite we may have, the human condition is a state of restless longing. If we pay close enough attention to the emptiness inside, it reveals itself to be a desire for closeness with our maker:

> You, God, are my God;
> earnestly I seek you;
> I thirst for you,
> my whole being longs for you,
> in a dry and parched land
> where there is no water.
> (Psalm 63:1)

Bare, black branches, stark against a scarlet sunset, like a Jan Pieńkowski painting. I love winter landscapes, where earth and sky merge together in a palette of purple and blue-grey, red and brown, and a stillness like sleep lies over everything. Winter skies are the best of all, especially at that moment when pale, watery light yields to soft, starlit darkness, and sharp silhouettes slip silently into the shadows.

Yet they speak so much of death, or at least of life arrested. Trees, shrubs and plants, woods, meadows, hedgerows and gardens stripped back to skeletal remnants of summer's glory; passive, and resisting, apparently resigned to short twilight days of gnawing cold and unforgiving winds. Winter comes to us in other ways too, sometimes in its season, anticipated and prepared for, sometimes stealing in unannounced, upsetting the precarious equilibrium of our carefully controlled lives, blowing cold, unwelcome draughts into corners we thought were double-glazed. However, just as creation itself follows patterns laid down in the infinite wisdom of a loving Creator, so the seasons come to us always in the context of the Father's love, fulfilling purposes of which only he is aware.

In 1995, we left a much-loved home and a country we had adopted as our own for twelve years to embark on twenty months of adventure and uncertainty. The children, all at boarding schools in the UK by that time, responded to the challenge with remarkable faith and humour. The lifestyle that ensued was not without considerable compensations: family time taking place in a marvellous kaleidoscope of cross-cultural settings, new friendships and interesting experiences burgeoning on all sides. Nevertheless, it took courage for the children to learn how to respond to simple questions like, 'Where do you live? or, 'What do your parents do?'

I had always relied quite heavily on being surrounded by my own family in my own home in order to be sure of who I am and what I do. So taking on a new international role within

A Rocha with no home base beyond a bulging suitcase and a borrowed car, and rather long periods of separation from the family, presented a significant challenge. Briefly we toyed with notions of 'homelessness', momentarily testing out the dramatic and slightly tragic overtones of the word, before rejecting the thought, ashamed to have entertained it even fleetingly. Such an idea is wholly inappropriate, outrageous even, for us to apply to ourselves in a world where countless millions are not only without homes, but also without hope. So 'multi-homed' became our chosen epithet and the privileged reality of the next year and a half. Hard questions remained, though. What is my true identity when the Lord removes those things I had thought were fundamental to the issue? And, more importantly, how could we provide a secure and stable home for our family while embracing a highly mobile life for a while? Certainly, the stripping back had begun. Stage one was the letting go, not only of the children, but also of greatly loved people and places in Portugal.

Going back to those winter trees, though . . . they may look dead; indeed, the part that is visible above the surface of the earth leaves us in little doubt. Below the surface, however, is a network of roots more extensive by far than the overarching latticework of branches which takes our breath away against the blazing winter sky. Out of sight, moisture and nutrients are sought and found to sustain the life of the tree through the weeks and months of coldness and exposure.

During that time, I often reflected on Jeremiah 17:7–10 about the tree planted by the water, as physical uprootedness caused me to examine where my roots actually are. I knew where they should be, yet the sense of vulnerability, so acute at times, and occasionally almost overwhelming, led me to discover that I was less rooted in Christ, less prepared to find my identity in him than I had thought. Only by God's grace, and then very gradually, was it possible to choose the rock of being in Christ and to reject the shifting sands of imagined status, whether through job, home or family.

There used to be a fruitful fig tree behind the house at Cruzinha. In the summer it was covered by a thick canopy of broad leaves, among which the plum-purple figs ripened till the sides burst and the sweet juice flowed, drawing birds and insects to the banquet like pins to a magnet. In winter, a casual observer might have thought the log basket was the tree's only and obvious destiny. Yet suddenly in early March small green pads of leaf and fruit would appear year on year simultaneously on the gnarled and stubby branches.

> See! The winter is past;
> the rains are over and gone.
> Flowers appear on the earth;
> the season of singing has come.
> (Song of Songs 2:11–12)

Similarly, in the life of the believer who is planted by the waterside, sending out their roots by the stream, the one who is drinking deeply of the water of life offered by Jesus alone, periods of winter silence can and must give way to the symphony of spring. I'm so thankful that the Lord took me out of my depth over those long months, that he helped me face some of my insecurities and fears, and that he led us together safely through the minefield of uncertainties towards a future and a hope. Yes, the spring is coming.

MIRIAM'S STORY[8]

We'd all heard the stories about the Rabbi. They were passed around at synagogue, by the well, in the market. He was said to have powers to cure sickness of body and mind. Our neighbour's cousin said her friend had seen with her own eyes this Jesus command a cripple by the pool of Bethesda to just stand up, and he did. And it wasn't just the miracles. His teaching got people talking, arguing about what he meant. It filled them with either hope or dismay, either way provoking a strong reaction. He was the most exciting thing in Israel.

It was a quiet life under the Romans, trying not to cause a scene, trying to get by. Other children in our village didn't complain, but I was always hoping something might happen to break the tedium. And it obviously wasn't just me feeling like that – all it took was for someone to say they'd heard this man was in a boat heading to our side of the lake and it was chaos. Everyone dropped what they were doing and we were going, almost all of us, to find him.

On the main road there were crowds, the kind of numbers you get going to Jerusalem for Passover. It was early summer, and all the feet kicked up so much dust it was like walking in a sand-coloured cloud for us children, nearer the ground as we were. I remember my eyes becoming crusty and dry and how I spat on my hand to try to clean away the grit.

Some people had been following the Rabbi a long time. I felt jealous, hearing them talk about seeing healings, demons cast out, wine made out of water. But it was okay, we wouldn't miss out completely. We would get to see him for ourselves now. I hoped he would do some miracles.

I held on to my father's cloak and made sure I didn't let my younger sister's hand go. Our mother was ahead of us – in that moment I'm not sure anyone would have noticed if we'd got lost.

And then we were by the lake shore in a crush of people. Everyone was shouting, pushing. He was on the boat that had just landed. He was there!

Two of the men with him pushed a path through the crowd, and then we were all following him as he led the way inland and uphill, the lake laid out behind us, a shimmery blue sheet. When he stopped, we spread out around him on the hillside, sitting on the scrubby grass and waiting expectantly to hear what he would say.

After a short while, Ruth was restless and said she was hungry. I looked around to show her I was trying to do something, but I knew we had left without provisions. I told her to chew on some grass and stop distracting me. I wanted to listen.

It was nothing like synagogue, where time hung heavy and my mind wandered over everything but the Scriptures. I didn't follow everything Jesus said, but I was captivated nonetheless. His stories made me laugh; he made me feel like running miles at top speed one moment and curling into a ball the next. My mother and father didn't take their eyes off his face. I had never seen them still and attentive like this before, and it didn't ever happen again afterwards.

Before we knew it, the sun was low in the sky. There was a lull and the Rabbi and his followers were talking among themselves. As though waking from deep sleep, our group stretched, paced, began to think about going home. And I realised I was ravenous, more than I have ever been. However dull my life, I wouldn't complain about my regular meals. I've never wanted food this badly and not known where to get it. I didn't like the feeling. My stomach growled and cramped, my head was achy and all I could think about was stuffing my face with bread. I felt furious with my parents for bringing me and Ruth so far from home without a way to feed us.

I know you might find this next part hard to believe. All these years later I do too, but I was there, and I tell you, it happened. A boy – he looked like he was about my age – was led by one

31

of the Rabbi's followers to the centre of the group. There was a hush and the Rabbi lifted something into the air and we heard him pray a blessing. Then the men asked us to sit clustered in groups. My mother pulled me and Ruth close. We all felt this sense of anticipation. Somehow Jesus was going to provide a meal. There was no doubt in any of our minds.

Much later, when the stars were out, we joined the trickle of others from our village heading down the hillside and home. We had feasted, absolutely feasted, on barley bread and fish. Not just us, but everyone who was there that day. Where did that bread and fish come from? I couldn't tell you, other than to describe what my eyes saw – Jesus, handing out more and more, until we were begging, through laughter, for him to stop. I will never forget it. I remember it with every hunger pang. There was so much food we left what we couldn't eat sitting there on the ground. Afterwards we heard the disciples had gathered it up – twelve whole basketfuls of leftovers.

My family were among those who rose early and made the journey around the lake the next day to find him. There were many of us, mostly those who had experienced the miracle meal. Even at the age of eleven I could tell he wasn't entirely pleased to see us. All I'd seen on his face the day before was kindness, a warmth from his eyes and a smile that made you feel like you were his favourite person. Now he looked frustrated, and he said, 'You only came to find me because I gave you bread. That kind of bread gives you very temporary satisfaction. You should have come after me because I can feed you food that will keep you alive forever.'

I am still trying to understand his next words, I think they are probably the most important words I will ever hear: 'I am the bread of life. Whoever comes to me will never go hungry. Whoever eats the flesh of the Son of Man and drinks his blood has eternal life, and I will raise them up in the last day.'

A PRAYER FOR THOSE WHO HUNGER

Jesus, Bread of Life, you knew extreme hunger when
you fasted those forty days in the desert. And you
know hunger is a daily reality for so many. You have
asked us, your people, to care about that as you do.

May those of us who have much be generous in
sharing and grateful for the plenty we enjoy.

Lord, sustain and nourish those who have
little, by the power of your Holy Spirit.

Amen.

Miranda's journals

1983–1984

29 September 1983

It is quite unnatural to wake up in a house so tidy and so clean. Everyone was awake by 6.30 a.m. and preserving at least a modicum of normality in otherwise totally abnormal circumstances. We solemnly drank a mug of tea, and the children munched apples. We had breakfast at Sally's – bacon and eggs like yesterday. For all of us the tension has been steadily mounting, and never has a goodbye been so prolonged. However, eventually all was packed and ready.

What a wrench it was to finally wave goodbye to so many dear friends. Many people came to the airport with packets of sweets for the children, a red rose for my buttonhole, bags of goodies and biscuits and big posters reading 'A Rocha – God go with you' held high.

It should have felt momentous, atmospheric, exciting – in a way it did, to be actually starting at last on this adventure given to us so many months ago – but I felt mainly weary, dazed and a little numb.

The journey was uneventful and the children very well behaved. There was some turbulence and a beautiful sunset. Elaine had packed little presents in our rucksacks, including dolls with hair for Jo and Esther ('What I *always* wanted,' said Jo).

We read the cards we had been given. Ed copied out for us Isaiah 55:12:

For you shall go out with joy
and be led forth in peace;
the mountains and the hills before
you shall break forth into singing,
and all the trees of the field shall clap their hands.[1]

And so we arrived at Faro airport at 7.30 p.m. to a warm, fragrant evening, and a big smile from our friend Tom who was waiting for us. Somehow we had no problems with customs, and despite being substantially in excess of our baggage allowance, we were not required to pay extra. Miraculously, Tom neatly packed the six of us (five Harrises and Ali who is helping with the children for our first year), six suitcases, assorted bags, rucksacks, photographic equipment, double buggy and five large sleeping bags into his battered Renault 4 and off we went to Lagoa where Edite was waiting. By 11.00 p.m. we were sitting round the table eating bread and jam and drinking coffee, with Jo, Esther and Jeremy tucked into bed on the floor, hardly able to believe we were here at last.

1 October 1983

Moving day, and we were deposited in our new lodgings. I set to make it homely. Joy's beautiful batik looks superb over the sofa, and Pauline's poster near the window. Jo has her own bedroom for the first time ever and is overjoyed. We have a little yard outside the tiny kitchen, which is crawling with ants, but in other respects cosy and delightful. Other livestock encountered so far include three large cockroaches and a number of mosquitoes which have attacked my face. Pete has been left in peace.

Tom and Edite arrived just before lunch and we set off to the about-to-close supermarket for weekend provisions and to the covered market for fruit and vegetables – similar to English ones but with additions such as pumpkins, figs and almonds. The kind old lady was very taken with Jem and gave him an orange and a pear. It is so frustrating to have no language as yet at our command, but it will come. We had lunch all together at Café Sumol on the seafront: chicken and chips, though not the kind we're used to. This was a gastronomic experience with garlic and spices and distinctive charcoal-grilled flavour.

3 October 1983

This is Jo's day. Today she starts in Class 2 at the International School with Mrs Smith as her teacher. All went very smoothly. Jo even brought homework back, which we did together after supper. I made a photograph chart for her bedroom while she was out, like the one we have in the main room, but with all her special friends and family featured.

I bought our first plant, a beautiful fern, which sits in the archway between the kitchen and living room. I'd love to get one for the top of the heavy wooden dresser too.

We went to the beach after meeting Jo off the bus, but the children were all tired and fractious, so we soon came home for stew and baked potatoes, stories and bedtime.

9 October 1983

Morning worship was on the beach today, built around the parable of the owner of the vineyard, with a big sand model as a visual aid. It was a good time and exhilarating to worship out of doors in such beautiful surroundings. After lunch everyone slept, and having put a sausage pie in the oven, we walked out along the beach, eastwards, past the fishing boats, collecting treasures in plastic buckets.

10 October 1983

It was 11.00 a.m. by the time I sat down at the table with my verbs in front of me, having queued at the bank and the post office. The Portuguese don't believe in queueing, so progress is slow for those of us who do – mostly grumbling English women on holiday! I also stopped at the market where our friend slipped a handful of almonds, a few grapes, a couple of tangerines and a pear into my bag in addition to the things I actually bought.

Esther and Jem went off to the hot beach very happily with Ali, coming back for lunch. Esther was eager to show me the blood on her knee which she had cut on a stone.

Pete returned at about 6.00 p.m. after quite an exciting day. Not only did they record forty-eight species of birds on the headland but also large numbers of swallowtail butterflies and, more importantly to us, a superb spot with a derelict cottage. The possibilities are building up again. Talking to Tom later, Pete said he was wondering about us moving into vacant properties on their own estate near Lagoa, as work from the headland would take at least eighteen months once started. There are no existing supplies of electricity or water. We must keep praying and wait to see the Lord opening the way up before us.

12 October 1983

Ali had a disastrous morning! She broke the buggy, dropped a bottle in the supermarket, only got four potatoes instead of a kilo, couldn't get ham and got charged about three times too much for the bread. Pete and I studied together in our bedroom as our cleaner Maria Alice was finishing off in the living room. She says her husband is a fisherman and that next week she will bring us a fish and show us how to cook it.

13 October 1983

We borrowed Tom's car this morning and had a glorious time near Faro on the lagoons and marshes. We saw all kinds of waders, white stork, kingfisher, fantail warblers and many others, and all the while could hear the gentle, companionable plop of abundant fish jumping in the pools. On our way back we gave a lift to a couple of young hitchhikers, Lennie and Jill from Oxford of all places, and had a good talk. Lennie is a half-baked Buddhist with lots of dotty ideas about life but very likeable, wild and rebellious. Jill has a Christian sister who, she says, has changed dramatically since she came to Christ. She was perhaps more thoughtful and open. We brought them home for a hot bath and a meal.

14 October 1983

This is the much-anticipated day on which we are due to go to the headland, and to the spot Pete and Les discovered with a derelict cottage on it, perfect for the centre. And yet today I feel weary, flat and discouraged. We went shopping in Portimão for about an hour. Esther and Jem had ice lollies and drank quantities of lemonade. We had a picnic lunch on the headland: the cottage is on a slight rise with a few trees and bushes around it. Northwards there is a beautiful view across a small valley to the Monchique hills; to the east the rough ground slopes down to the river estuary with the outskirts of Alvor beyond. There is even an avenue, albeit a rather uncertain one, of trees leading up to the cottage. We feel simultaneously excited and apprehensive at the possibilities for the place and the length of time it would take to establish a fully functional centre. The Lord knows.

In the evening Les led our fellowship meeting, which was excellent, based on Luke 2 and how God ordered events and intervened in the lives of powerful people to ensure that the birth of Jesus took place at the right time and in the right place. We feel there is a message for A Rocha there.

17 October 1983

A combination of mosquitoes with their sinister hum and Jeremy with his not at all sinister but rather highly cheerful shouting caused the day to burst upon us earlier than normal. After a good bowl of porridge, I took Jo up to the school bus. Another glorious morning.

We had our first visitors today, Keith and Celia Butterwell, and had a lovely afternoon together on the beach. Pete and Les had a fine day with a golden eagle on Monchique and Alpine swifts outside the International School. Keith and Celia stayed for a hilarious and chaotic children's bedtime, then we went up for a lovely supper with Les and Wendy (melon, chicken fricassee, and yoghurt and cream with fruit). Wendy had made the flat so warm and welcoming with plants, shells, flowers and assorted botanical trophies, with a candle on the table in a saucerful of shells and pebbles.

20 October 1983

Here begins the most difficult three days of this adventure so far. On Thursday, Les and Wendy, Peter and myself went for a cliff walk a little further along the coast, turning inland opposite the international school and walking for a couple of miles across spectacular clifftops, made alarmingly precarious by sudden potholes, partly concealed by bushes, plunging sometimes forty or fifty feet down to the sea below. In places you come upon these deathtraps quite frequently, arriving on the very brink before you are aware of waves pounding the cave walls below. In fact, one of the workmen who built Tom and Edite's house lost his life in this way just a few days after his contract with them had concluded. However, today was without incident, thankfully, and a glorious hot day. Wendy and Les shared their chicken pie with us for lunch.

On the return journey our discussions became heated and suddenly soared out of control, all of us losing our cool. Whatever the overt reasons, it was the inevitable release of tension that has been steadily building up in us all, not least owing to relatively trivial pressures of a practical kind to do with living here. Mutual misunderstanding and fear have arisen because we have not had enough time together to talk through the project on a fundamental level, nor time to get to know each other and build open, trusting relationships. Whatever the causes, as Les wisely remarked while we drank a calming cup of tea, it was a storm in a teacup, and even in the pain of it – because sessions of frank talking always are painful – we are aware that this is a good sign that the Lord must work in us before he can work through us and that these relationships at the heart of A Rocha must be established in a Christlike frame if we are to minister together.

25 October 1983

Today we woke up to crashing thunder and torrential rain, such that within half an hour the road outside was awash, flowing past the house like a river, and the backyard filled with about two inches of water on which floated assorted beachballs, spades and the like. We all felt exhilarated and acutely aware of what water means in a dry and dusty land. By breakfast time we were in the middle of a power cut, to the delight of Jo, Esther and Jem, eating our porridge and rolls by the light of a paraffin lamp and two candles.

I attempted some housework, made a stew and sorted out quantities of soggy washing. Our friend Paul from England joined us unexpectedly for lunch and mysteriously vanished afterwards — before the washing-up — reappearing equally mysteriously while coffee was brewing in the evening.

28 October 1983

More torrential rain which lasted most of the day, keeping the children homebound. Drilling is in progress next door, and also in the road outside: some sewage problem apparently. Our water supply was cut off briefly, but caused no great inconvenience except that Ali had to wash the fresh mackerel in rainwater. I was set upon by an Alsatian-type dog down by the market and bitten on the calf; there was no real physical damage but I must admit it shook me.

Les and Wendy came for lunch and to plan next week. We feasted on mackerel baked in garlic butter with mushrooms, cloves and peppercorns, artichokes fried with onions and almonds, and assorted veg.

29 October 1983

Conversation lesson today in which we learnt several useful phrases, for example: *Não attire contre mim. Estou a estudar pássaros; não quero incomodar nem fazer mal. O cão não morde?* – which being roughly translated means, 'Please don't shoot me. I'm only studying the birds and don't want to disturb you or do you any harm. Does your dog bite?'

30 October 1983

A beautiful, bright and fragrant morning. Jeremy and Esther flooded the bathroom — again — in a delightful game of paddling pools while I frantically hung all the damp, grey washing out for about the third time this week and attempted to repulse yet another invasion of ants. They are marching in columns around the walls in the pantry, kitchen and dining room and seem quite unperturbed by lashings of ant powder which Edite assures me is highly toxic. We'll probably die of poisoning before they do.

2 November 1983

Pete took Jo up to the school bus and Ali had the little ones so I had some quiet time to read and pray. I still haven't cracked that one: the Lord is the whole reason for being here, for being wherever we are, and yet it is as if I resent even five minutes to talk to him in an unhurried way, tending rather to ask him to bless my language study, letter-writing and housework and please understand that I feel a bit rushed and busy again today and can't really stop. There must be a solution, and I must find it, otherwise I'll be experiencing drought like the Algarve.

Ali had a happy morning with Esther and Jem, and Maria Alice cleaned half the house, which is the agreement now, as she couldn't manage to do it all in three hours. One of her idiosyncrasies, which I haven't worked out yet, is the habit of putting all the pillows away in cupboards!

Pete and I hope to make a decision about finding a new washing machine as ours has finally departed this life, having successfully turned almost all our clothes murky grey. We slipped out in the evening for a drink to discuss. We feel we are getting to know the waiters at Santola and enjoy practising our few sentences. It's nice to catch up on the events of the day.

8 November 1983

Went to the supermarket where I used both my Portuguese sentences and then to the market to buy fresh fish. Marie Alice arrived to say she wasn't coming to clean that day, but she came with me to the electric shop to find the mechanic who was due to come and mend the washing machine last Friday.

I took Esther and Jem to the café opposite for a lemonade mid-morning. They liked that and the dash there through pouring rain. In fact, it's been a good day for them, what with the lady in the supermarket giving them lollipops too. Esther started the day with gastronomic preoccupations, saying thoughtfully before breakfast, 'Why don't you try me on bubble gum, Mum?'

Jo had a fall at school and came back plastered in red antiseptic stuff, with bruising below the eye, but she had a happy evening learning a verse of a carol for homework and enjoyed *The Rainbow Garden* which I am reading to her at the moment. She has created an art gallery in her room by means of quantities of Blu Tack, attaching stories, assorted creatures and pictures, postcards and bits of ribbon et cetera to the wall behind her bed. I was cross about the damage to the paintwork. Ali and I had a good talk and pray later, both aware of the temptation to land on the children from a great height purely because of feeling under pressure oneself; also the tendency to say 'no' to their proposed projects because of the effort involved and hard work incurred. We resolve to do better.

4 January 1984

Our house investigations took us to many interesting places, not least a bleak five-bedroom scout hut reminiscent of a farm outbuilding. The owner plied us with glasses of ferociously powerful brandy which I narrowly escaped by pursuing the children across the vegetable patch. Tom has his own ways of dealing with these situations. 'Can we see the garden again?' he says innocently, and then under his breath to Pete, 'Watch this!' So saying, a quick jerk over his shoulder and the foul liquid is doing its worst to the potatoes.

5 January 1984

Family trip to Portimão and had a highly successful and enjoyable morning. The children enjoyed rushing around the covered market and going on the swings and seesaw opposite. We had lunch at the hamburger café. All very satisfactory. On the bus on the way home Jo befriended an old fisherman who gave us his entire bucket of fresh sardines, an act of generosity that moved us considerably.

After a rest at home we had an expedition along the beach to collect shells for the shell curtain we intend to put up in the new home. It was one of those magical times, the sea the most brilliant blue as the sun sank lower in the sky. I wonder if we have been grateful enough to God for placing us in this beautiful spot to start our Portuguese life. We had sardines, brown bread and vinho verde for supper.

18 January 1984

The two trustees arrived considerably earlier than expected today to find me barefooted slicing aubergines, mushrooms and peppers for the moussaka, and washing all over the living room. But as Ali sagely remarked, it's probably better that they should find us in an authentic shambles than in unnatural tidiness! Esther and Jem were delighted with these new potential storytellers and lost no time in finding a knee each to snuggle on.

24 January 1984

Our latest visitors hired a car for three days and today we did a round trip ending on the headland, where disconcertingly there appears to be a good deal of building going on on the western side, and much of the southern tip is being ploughed over. We had a coffee in 'our café' where Pete inadvertently spilt a whole coffee over himself having explained that we were going to be their next-door neighbours.

Our future landlady was warm and friendly, letting us show our friends around the flat and sending us off with a bag of lemons and a carnation for me.

15 February 1984
Esther woke up in the night saying she felt sick, I had nightmares, there was a violent thunderstorm and the children all woke at 5.45 – otherwise it was a good night. After the usual cold sweats and exam paralysis, I managed to get my third Portuguese test completed and met Pete at the café for time to prepare the Bible study. He had with him a difficult letter from our trustees, which contributed to the gloom. When we got home it was to find that Ali had made a lovely supper to cheer us up, which it did.

TWO

PREPARATION

*A little consideration, a little thought
for others, makes all the difference.*

EEYORE

Whether we give the task of preparing for guests at least a week or simply try to be at home at the agreed time has to do with upbringing, culture, theology, personality and life stage. I have friends who figure out sleeping arrangements at bedtime, and friends who make up beds with freshly laundered sheets days in advance. Both households are equally welcoming and warm: the former is always up for an impromptu overnighter, the latter guaranteed to provide the conditions for a deep and restorative sleep.

As our world becomes smaller, nations more multicultural and cultures more fragmented, no etiquette manual could ever hope to cover all eventualities. In lieu of a manual, then, a principle: preparing our houses, ourselves and our food rarely goes wrong when done in love – not just love for our visitor, but also for God and for his creation.

I will now give you the benefit of learning from (a small selection of) my mistakes. In the summer of 2018, Shawn was appointed as the vicar of four churches in villages on the edge of Bath. In the Church of England, housing is provided for church leaders. You have no choice, but, given a thousand houses to look at, I would have chosen this house. I immediately wanted to stack it with people, and we threw open invitations to the wind. Over a six-month period, we had guests staying for twenty-one weekends and untold numbers for meals. We had new people to get to know, long-term relationships to maintain and space to accommodate those in need – something as a family we try to do whenever possible.

This might have been manageable on top of regular work and life, but I had set standards for myself that ensured I ended up in a state of interminable, miserable exhaustion bordering on depression. My standards required beds to be made up, menus planned and the first meal made so I could be fully attentive to our visitors on arrival; they demanded clean bathrooms and children, a clutter-free entrance hall, atmospheric lighting and a wide range of hot and cold drinks on tap. They included a clause about physical and emotional availability for the duration of the stay, my own and ideally the whole family's. It was all quite hard work and, as the weeks went by, joyful anticipation was replaced by dread, regardless how beloved the next arrival.

Who was all this effort really for? The heart of hospitality is the care of another, and if I am brutally honest, what I was doing over those months was more about me. I was proud of our beautiful and spacious new home, which made me feel grown up and important. I wanted to offer the same quality of experience that my mother gave to those who came to her home. I wanted people to write gushing accolades in our guest book and for the next set of guests to read them and think nice thoughts about us. I wanted to believe I had the gift of hospitality, though I had forgotten hospitality can be far simpler.

One of my favourite children's books, *A Little Princess* by Francis Hodgson Burnett, is the story of a child called Sara Crewe who was sent from India to board in great luxury at Miss Minchin's London school for well-heeled girls. When her father died in penury, she was left a penniless orphan and became the servant of her former classmates, banished to a bare, freezing garret under the school eaves. Even in these drastically changed circumstances, Sara's warmth, integrity and imagination shone undimmed, and those she had welcomed into her plush and well-appointed suite in her former life continued to seek her out. All she now had to offer was a hard mattress, a bleak view of the grey city's rooftops and herself. At the end of physically and emotionally punishing days of demeaning labour, she repeatedly found the strength to tell stories, wipe tears and offer counsel. The story reminds me that any of us, in pretty much any situation, can host healing and joyful occasions from which we too can receive.

As with many things in life, there are extremes to the preparation stage of hospitality. At one end of the scale, it takes on such horrific proportions that the host is wrung out and shaky with exhaustion by the time the guest arrives; at the other, this stage is a matter of opening and shutting the fridge door and deciding a takeaway is perfectly acceptable. When Jesus and his disciples visited the home of his friends Mary and Martha, his admonishment to Martha might seem an endorsement of the low-key approach. Mary plonked herself down by Jesus' feet and hung on his words. Luke writes:

> Martha was distracted by all the preparations that had to
> be made. She came to him and asked, 'Lord, don't you
> care that my sister has left me to do the work by myself? Tell
> her to help me!'
>
> 'Martha, Martha,' the Lord answered, 'you are worried
> and upset about many things, but few things are needed
> – or indeed only one. Mary has chosen what is better, and
> it will not be taken away from her.'
> (Luke 10:40–42)

Jesus rarely issued one-size-fits-all dictates, and we'd be
mistaken to read this as a ruling that making dinner is wrong and
sitting around chatting is right. In this instance, Jesus could see
Martha's busyness and mounting stress depriving her of a
chance to spend some quality time with him – bearing in mind
he was the Messiah, the Son of God, under her roof for only a
few precious hours. If there is a principle here, it is this: we need
to ask ourselves, what is needed in this particular situation by this
particular person? What will make this encounter a blessing for
both of us? What is God's best intention for our time together
and how can I, given all the constraints, facilitate that?

I recently discovered that here in Bath it is considered optimal
to arrive nine minutes late. How we react if someone arrives
early, or even unexpectedly, tells us a lot about whether we
have grasped, as Mary had, what *really* matters.

On Tuesday the week began to go pear-shaped, and I realised
I'd have to overnight in London after my outpatient appointment instead of returning home, as I'd need to be back in the
hospital on Wednesday. But from the moment I heard
Rebecca's voice on the phone that morning to her goodbye

inside the hospital next day, I felt wrapped up in this family's extraordinary love. There are eight bedrooms in their huge, rambling Victorian house, solidly built in 1880. Though in North London, it is framed by a garden so luxuriant and semi wild that you feel you've tumbled into deep English countryside.

I landed on them at perhaps the worst possible moment, with sixteen dinner guests arriving that evening, most of them psychiatrists, and yet they made me feel like a favourite guest. I was given a lovely airy room, double bed, fabulous dinner and the unexpected joy of sensational cheese for breakfast. We had lots of unhurried chats and laughter and catching up despite the many other people they were surrounded by. The best gift of all was the brilliant and vivid reminder that it is possible to incarnate kingdom, to live a life of love that embraces everyone, which puts important things on top of the pile and is free to walk away from all the trivia of modern life. All of a sudden, I have a lot to think about.

'When I get married, my house will never look like this.' The words hung dangerously in the air between us, the seventeen-year-old and me. I surveyed the debris of my kitchen, stunned by the comment, and was dismayed to register some justification for it in the sea of unwashed coffee mugs and general flotsam and jetsam and of teatime for three very small offspring. I didn't want my home to look like this either. Like my friend who began married life ironing everything in sight, including her husband's socks, I had high ideals for homemaking. But, always quick to leap to my own defence, I pointed out that in spite of the fact that the latest baby had only arrived a few weeks earlier, the pace of life had not slowed, the door had remained open to all comers (including the dozen or so youth group members currently making coffee-coloured rings on the furniture), and being a domestic slave was not part of the deal. It rankled. And yet even before the ruffled feathers had settled back into some semblance of order, I realised the remark carried within it a small seed of success. We had resolved to be *real* – to be known as we really were, not as we wished we were. If this is vital in building a relationship with God, surely it is equally fundamental to human discourse.

We had not been in the parish long when the episode just described took place. The process of creating a home for the family and for those we hoped to help through our church work was still underway. In those days, when a curate's salary didn't stretch too far, we would pray for shoes for the kids rather than go out to buy them, and we were grateful for the bags of unwanted clothes deposited intermittently inside the front porch by charitable church members.

The lack of funds was an issue for me. I had grown up surrounded by fine antique chests and tables which my parents had mostly inherited. Thus, as well as being objects of useful-ness and elegance, they were imbued with a stabilising sense of family history and continuity. The walls of our various homes, as well as being tastefully painted, were festooned with original etchings and paintings similarly acquired, and the many shelves were laden with rank upon rank of books to suit every intellect and satisfy every interest. Everything cohered in aesthetic and practical harmony.

Although our new home was an attractive and generously proportioned semi-detached from the 1950s, I was frustrated by how little I could do to transform the inside. I hated the frantically patterned carpets, the tatty Formica kitchen units, the huge mirrors in every upstairs room concealing whole walls and probably original fireplaces too. And I hated our motley collection of second-hand furniture which we were obliged to arrange around the house. I resented the fact I couldn't buy bright scatter cushions, matching curtains or even plants to beautify our home. I had inherited and unwittingly nurtured some unhealthy ideas about homemaking and found myself straining towards an unattainable idea of achieving a family environment in which good taste, quality materials, tidiness and cleanliness miraculously combined to project an image of calm and competency.

I was still too insecure to realise that none of this matters at all. Coordinating colour schemes and quality furniture are not the criteria by which a house becomes a safe and welcoming home. In fact, the trappings can be – and so often are – the single greatest barrier to genuine communication and the stirrings of friendship. Instead of the disarming smile that dissolves a stranger's nervousness, we smile brightly and deliver a conflicted message: 'Do come in! (But don't feel at home, just admire it and know that your own will never match up.)' Simply put, my need was for people, not things; to belong, not to set myself apart by my different background and cultural clutter; to confess my needs, not disguise them by superficial redecorating. It wasn't just the house we lived in that needed attention; it was the house of my life.

Renovation is a messy business, and building community is a messy business too. Instinctively we keep up appearances in front of people we don't know well so that no one will detect the pitiful papering over painful fissures, which, like cracked heels, inflict discomfort and hamper mobility. We long for intimacy and find ourselves instead prolonging the opposite. We long to be known as we are, yet are terrified of that very thing becoming apparent. We would rather be a museum piece to be admired than a work in progress to be pushed, pressed, chipped and moulded into shape.

Self-exposure is never easy, as Philip Yancey reminds us in his book on prayer: 'but when I do it I learn that underneath the layers of grime lies a damaged work of art that God longs to repair'.[1] In so doing we enable others also to lower their own masks without fear of rejection or judgement. And below them we discover something vulnerable and beautiful too. So we draw closer to one another in our mutual transparency instead of driving each other away by intimidating projections of perfection. Knowing and being known involves a painful journey, demanding much courage to face ourselves and perseverance going forward, navigating the disappointments and misunderstandings common to everyone.

The slow realisation that our rather haphazard homemaking might actually be a help not a hindrance set me thinking more creatively about how I might find the place I so craved in the church community. I couldn't often make it to the evening service, where exciting new signs of spiritual life were beginning to appear, or to the dynamic youth group, almost a hundred strong, which met afterwards. In the mornings it was often my turn to supervise the crèche, so Sunday evenings could find me feeling more excluded and lonely than ever. Gradually it dawned on me that I was not the only person on this particular beach and, after a while of drifting helplessly in and out with the turning of each tide, I invited a few neighbours to join me once a week for some exploration of the Bible and a little relief from the narrow confines of our own homes. I doubt whether our conversations were particularly stimulating or even very coherent, but empathy, warmth and the beginning of trust were born and began to grow among us.

I also began, a little hesitantly it must be said, to invite people round for meals. At first this presented a huge challenge to my confidence. I knew how to talk to three-year-olds, although Jo was often several jumps ahead of me, and I had plenty of party pieces to fall back on in their company, but how do you talk intelligently to twenty- or thirty-somethings about politics, music or current affairs when 'Old McDonald had a farm' is taking up the largest space in your brain?

One evening, several of our new friends from church came over for dinner. I planned the meal carefully, invested hours in meticulous food preparation and anguished over what to wear. With the brisk efficiency of a military campaign, I got the children ready for bed and managed to be at the door when the guests arrived, if not dressed to kill at least without the children's food all over my jumper. The evening was a success. What we talked about has long ago vanished in the midst of a million words and a thousand subsequent conversations, but I remember thinking I'd held my end up. As the evening drew to a convivial close, and still feeling reassured that I could handle adult company after all, I helped one friend on with her coat. So far so good. Then, to her astonishment and my absolute horror, I found myself buttoning it up for her as well!

My parents' home was always atmospheric, full of music, light, ready laughter and human warmth. When people came to stay, Mum's preparation included leaving a carefully chosen pile of books by the bed, a welcome card on the pillow, flowers from the garden on the windowsill. Each detail was small, but they added up to an impression – an impression that she was glad you were there.

I am the first to say we can't all be Mirandas and I am not suggesting we try to mimic her style. But we can all be inspired by what she accomplished in making people feel loved. The place to start is by prayerfully bringing our guests to mind. What do we know about them, their way of life, the burdens they carry and the things that bring them comfort and pleasure? If they are struggling to cope and their own home environment is chaotic, they might be heartened to find our kitchen sink full of dirty dishes. If they come from a culture where hospitality must be reciprocated and are struggling to make ends meet, it may be a great relief to them to be served a tin of soup and some cheese on toast, something they could hope to match. If they have a dairy intolerance, a stash of oat milk will communicate love as effectively as any more traditional gesture. This is something Shawn has taught me. For him, the kind of hospitality that puts him most at ease and that he therefore prefers to offer goes something like: 'Here is the fridge. Here is where we keep the rest of the food. Help yourself.'

THE ETHICS OF CONSUMPTION

An important part of preparing to offer hospitality is procuring the ingredients for the food you plan to serve. This might seem simple on the face of it – make a list, go to a shop or log on to your supermarket of choice and get the items you need. But there are many constraints and choices to be made and, far from being simple, shopping for food is about as morally and intellectually complex as it gets.

Money was tight for our family while I was growing up, and more often than not there were many more than the six of us sitting down to eat. Until a certain point, however, we ate a varied and abundant range of foods. Then came the day someone made the mistake of giving Mum a book: *The Food We Eat*[2] – or as we came to call it, *The Food We Used to Eat* –by investigative food journalist Joanna Blythman. In it she makes a compelling case for considering not just price but also the well-being of producers, the skill and care taken over how food is grown, reared or caught and the impact of what we eat on the soil, air and water. She led us over the seldom-crossed chasm between farm and fork, and with knowledge came responsibility. The holder of the household budget now knew the desperate plight of the attractively priced battery chickens. We would henceforth only eat the happiest of birds, and only on the rare occasions we could afford them. Mum became equally enlightened about beef, pork and a seemingly ever-growing list of other consumables, from chocolate to kiwi fruit, eggs to pasta. I hold Joanna Blythman personally responsible for the abomination that is Shepherd's Beany Pie, which made its unwelcome appearance at far too many of my childhood dinner times. For a while we 'suffered with vegetarianism' – a phrase I discovered recently while googling whether my newly veggie daughter could eat Turkish delight (yes, it is indeed suitable for those suffering with vegetarianism, the website earnestly informed me). Meat was back on the menu in less-straitened times, but always formerly happy meat.

We talk a lot in A Rocha about 'joining the dots' – the ongoing exercise of connecting facets of life that are artificially segregated: prayer from work from worship; money from soil from flavour; humans from nature from God. Perhaps we need reminding that the business of food shopping is profoundly spiritual and imbued with relational consequences.

Community includes not only the people around us, but also the creation itself. We all live in creation and handle its raw material every day. We didn't even have our own day in the story of creation. We arrived on day six along with 'livestock, the creatures that move along the ground, and the wild animals' (Gen. 1:24). We are part of creation, not outside it or over it or above it.

We can't opt in or out of creation care or take it up as a hobby, like gardening or golf, if we aren't too busy. We are doing it already – badly or well, living our relationship with

God's world like his children who love him, or like people who don't know that it was made with infinite care, love and delight.

Care begins with noticing. Anything God makes deserves our attention. Careful observation leads to wonder, worship and giving thanks. Our task is to find a place within creation and to worship the one by whom, through whom and for whom it was all made (Col. 1:15–17).

When my niece Jessica was three, her parents took her to see cows being milked. She watched, entranced, as the huge, placid beasts stood patiently in a row while the milking apparatus throbbed rhythmically up and down on their udders, carrying white fluid through various tubes and eventually out of sight. Finally, and thoughtfully, she said, 'Are they putting it in or taking it out?' Sometimes we become disastrously separated from creation. We all recognise the white stuff in our lattes or on our breakfast cereal but fail to connect it with anything other than a plastic bottle or carton.

IN PRAISE OF FOOD PREP

Why is it that, in a world where cookbooks frequently appear on bestseller lists and chefs become celebrities, we spend less time cooking than ever before? Perhaps it is because time has become our most precious commodity and we are loath to spend it on something as mundane as peeling a potato or crushing a clove of garlic. Many businesses have sprung up on the basis of that assumption, delivering meals in their component parts, chopped, washed, weighed and ready for assemblage and cooking. Grocery stores carry ever-increasing numbers of 'convenience items' – you no longer have to dice onions, chop chillies, cube beef or make pastry, stock or any kind of mess in the kitchen if you don't want to.

But, as with hunger, avoiding what may seem on the face of it unpleasant or taxing brings great losses along with the gains. Shortcutting the process of creating a meal from scratch robs you of that feeling you get when you give a gift into which you have poured a part of yourself, and robs the recipient of the moment of wonder as they understand they are worth more to you than they realised. Avoiding food preparation means depriving yourself of an intense sensory experience, the sharp tang that hits the back of your throat as you slice into a lemon, the chalky grit of an eggshell, the deep purple of a beet that stains your fingers hot fluorescent pink. If we slow ourselves down and pay attention, God's creative genius is evident in the variety, the riot of taste, texture and colour. The knife and the chopping block, the wok and the steamer – who knew these dull, domestic items could call us to worship as persuasively as a priest with a prayer book?

Here is a suggestion for consideration: that to the extent we are able, we seek out the very best ingredients to prepare and serve up – the ones with the fullest flavour, the most vibrant colours, brought to market by people who care for the earth. That we savour the experience of peeling, chopping, mincing, slicing, mixing, roasting, frying, steaming. That we do not begrudge the extra pennies, the extra minutes, the burden of care, but offer them up from generous, full hearts, a sacrifice of praise.

ATEN'S STORY[3]

In the heat of the day, everything at our camp is quiet and still – even the leaf beetles stop scuttling around and the flies settle. For all the discomfort of the sun's full blaze, it's my favourite time. My work begins in the dark, rebuilding the fires, walking to the well for water, feeding the animals, all before the older servants are even awake. By the time the midday meal has been cleared I ache from head to foot sole, my long hair sticking to my neck with sweat. And then, like everyone else, I can rest a while.

On this particular day I had gone to sit under the oaks, out of sight so no one would see me and remember something I hadn't done. There is always something. I had my back to the trunk of one of the biggest trees, and the shade beneath was dense enough for the light beyond to dazzle my eyes. So I heard them first, their voices low and portentous as a grumble of thunder.

My whole body tensed, muscle memory throwing suddenly clenched fists involuntarily up to chest height: my brother's posture when I provoke him. He'd laugh at me, a skinny girl facing down three grown men alone. But he would have understood. We'd been with Abraham since we were children and were seldom beaten, but we both remembered Egypt. The sound of strangers was the sound of danger, and for a moment fear robbed me of my breath.

The strangers halted a stone's throw from my tree. They stood still, taking in the camp, waiting quietly and patiently in the full sun for someone to see them. I looked frantically for a way to get back to the tents unnoticed to raise the alarm. The distance was short but entirely exposed, and I knew I would have to find cour-age and run for it in full view. But then, the Lord be praised, Abraham himself was approaching, hand shading his eyes, his weathered form supported by a stick.

He propelled himself towards the men as fast as he was able, and then, to my astonishment, he was bending at the waist, kneeling, bowing on the ground before them. 'Please,' he said, 'do me the great honour of breaking your journey with us. We can fetch water so you can wash your feet.' (And let me tell you, they needed washing. I could smell them.) 'Then you can rest under this tree while we prepare some food so you are refreshed.'

Why was I hoping they would agree? Of course, if they hadn't, it would have been a great insult to my master, to our whole household. But there was more to it, more than the chance of a diversion from the daily routine, more than the likelihood of a feast with leftovers enough for even us servants – there was something about the strangers that overcame my fear and made me want to step out of the shadows and move closer. By the time they had conferred and turned to clasp Abraham's hands, to nod and smile, I was there behind him, and their smiles embraced me too.

Turning to hurry back to the tent, Abraham nearly fell over me. 'Aten! What are you doing here? Run – tell Sarah to use three seahs of the best flour to bake bread. Help her with the kneading and make sure the coals are hot. And if you see your brother, ask him to meet me by the cattle.'

I was halfway there already, tripping in my excitement, the weariness of the long morning forgotten. He was going all out – this was going to be a meal of mammoth proportions.

For the next few hours, as the newly clean men reclined by the trees, the household was a buzz of activity. I caught the mournful lowing as the mother of the chosen calf protested his removal from her side, the scrape of the knives sharpened on the rock, the shouts from the boys straining to lift the carcass onto the butchering bench, Abraham's old man voice straining to issue orders: 'Fetch more water. Keep that fire going. Curds! Milk!'

I felt a shiver of fear all of a sudden. We'd be making considerable dents in our carefully hoarded stores of food, and who knew if the next rains would come, or if our cows would stay healthy? But, like everyone else, I was soon caught up again in the fever of preparation and did not fret for long.

It was dusk by the time the food was heaped on platters, ready to serve. Holding oil lamps, a small procession of men took our offerings and placed them on the ground by our guests before retreating a few steps away, allowing them to eat in peace. The air was fragrant with fresh bread and roasted meat, settling dust and herbs, and the early stars almost as bright as the lamps. It was new moon and the night would be dark.

I was in Sarah's tent, sweeping the flour from the floor, laying out the sleeping mats and coverings when I heard her laugh – a short, sharp burst, sour as milk forgotten in the sun. I crept closer, wondering what could have provoked such a sound. It wasn't until the next day I heard that these visitors had promised my wizened, ancient mistress a babe in arms within the year. What I did hear, though, was Sarah saying, 'I did not laugh.' I knew better.

So now we are all waiting, watching her stomach. We've been here before, watching Sarah's stomach until Hagar's was too large to ignore. This time feels different. Those men smiled at me, and I know they were angels at the very least.

A PRAYER FOR WHEN YOU ARE COOKING

Holy God, I want to be a holy cook.

As I collect my ingredients, let me be attentive to the bounty of all you have made to nourish our bodies. Sharpen my hazy sight to see the colours, shapes and patterns piled on my counter.

Let the work of peeling, paring, chopping, sorting all be done in glad service of those my labour will bless.

As the heat does its part and flavours fill the air, fill me with your Holy Spirit. Prepare me as I prepare this meal.

Amen.

Miranda's journals

1985–1993

3 July 1985

Tearful farewells to Fi, who has become such a friend to us all the months she was with us following Bethan's birth. She leaves us a host of happy memories as well as an organised domestic routine, such that washing, ironing and baking can all be kept up to date during the week following her departure.

10 July 1985

Jem's fifth birthday started early with a perky voice saying, 'Open the blinds – it's all mouldy in here!' Much excitement over the model plane from Granny and Grandpa and assorted trucks from us. The highlight of the day came in the evening with a trip to the Italian ice cream house in Portimão, everyone dressed up to the nines for the occasion. We all ate extra-immense ice creams in glasses: meals in themselves and a wildly extravagant celebration given the eye-watering price tag.

On our return home, Señhora Maria arrived with a lovely bunch of flowers for Jem. He was evidently moved – 'Are they really for *me*?' – and wanted to put them straight in his room.

17 July 1985

I am much preoccupied at the moment with the matter of lifestyle and the plight of the poor and the injustices of a society that is geared to making the rich richer and neglecting the poor. Jesus clearly identified with the latter, to the extent of being born in a filthy stable, and was always to be found among them. I wonder how we can do the same and live out our lives here in active compassion for the underprivileged. It is a small gesture, but from today we are giving up butter. A pitifully small gesture.

We are also giving up sweets for different reasons. This morning was spent in the dentist's surgery having a badly decayed tooth extracted. The options were to have it out or embark on very costly root canal treatment. I must admit thoughts on all the above played quite a part in opting for the former, though instinctively of course one would prefer to hold on to all one's teeth. Again, a pitifully small gesture which will affect no one but maybe just a step in the right direction.

After Pete's four fillings last week, it is worth recording that the whole family are reformed characters as regards tooth cleaning. Life has become an endless round of meticulous circular brushing, dental floss and eager grimacing into mirrors to check the effect of all this enthusiasm.

11 August 1985

The pace of life is so fast now it's hard to keep up! This week we've had two sleeping on the flat roof, one on Jem's floor, another on the girls' floor and someone on the sofa in the sitting room.

22 August 1985

The hottest day we can remember. Jo, Estie and Jem had a prolonged water fight after lunch. Very sensible in these temperatures. Señhora Maria came up with a basket of figs and a little melon for Jem. Poor dear lady is badly bereaved and adrift after Joaquim's death. On Tuesday I went to visit her with Estie, taking some flowers and oranges, and she talked without stopping for about twenty minutes. She shared stories with us about her husband and family and her own childhood, and talked a lot of faith and heaven. We prayed together and left with a bowl of green figs from her trees for the children. She is a marvellous person and full of courage.

28 August 1985

We went into Portimão to make decisions about tiles and cabinets for the kitchen and to Cruzinha to decide where to put them. It looks beautiful as ever in the bright sunshine, but we were horrified and disgusted by the state it is in – filth everywhere, rubbish piled in great mounds at the bottom of the garden, and smelly too. It's almost unbelievable that people can live like that. We are all the more impatient to start the clearing-up operations and to get it into shape.

16 September 1985

Very happy two-week visit from Mum and Dad and so sad to see them go. Little Bethan again angelic all day, lying in her basket on a marble shelf by our table at lunch and sleeping on the coffee table afterwards, chatty and smiley in her buggy and a bit amazed by the rain, having never seen it before. She didn't cry once – in fact, Dad remarked towards the end of the week that he didn't think he'd heard her cry at all. What a remarkable baby.

25 April 1986

We have been in Cruzinha for four dizzy weeks. On the move day, within five minutes of the vans drawing up, two visiting botanists were dissecting orchids in the front room, while removal men passed with chests of drawers, beds and so on. Friends were due to arrive at 11.00 p.m., and once the children were settled, we all began to unload the boxes and load the bookcases. We eventually went to bed around 3.00 a.m., leaving the lights on, and at 5.30 a.m. woke up startled to find a cheery builder in our bedroom! Everyone got up and we all had tea.

So began what was surely the busiest fortnight of our lives, with Easter to celebrate, two study groups staying nearby and countless visitors streaming through each day, as well as painters, carpenters, plumbers, electricians and builders all setting the place to rights. By Saturday night we had hot water, albeit bright red, and the following week glass was put in our bathroom windows. We have watched the extension grow, the shutters transform into brilliant blue, the rooms gleam with fresh paint, and with great joy we have seen from our kitchen window twelve bee-eaters prospecting for nest sites. Yesterday a beautiful, dark chestnut refectory table, a hundred years old from northern Portugal, was delivered. I don't regret spending half the furnishing budget on this one item!

We've adopted a thin, wormy, lame dog we've named Bonita and have already grown to love her.

31 May 1986

At lunchtime I found a large snake at the bottom of the stairs; I don't know which of us was more scared. Also a large centipede appeared in the kitchen sink, about 2½ inches long. This place is getting too buggy for me. Eight students failed to turn up and our assistant wardens, Mark and Frank, came back to sleep on the floor, unable to get past the guard dog into their village accommodation.

22 June 1986

Peter worked incredibly hard felling the eucalyptus, branch by branch, and putting in the citrus. Our volunteers Luis and Zé left yesterday before the hard work began, after much showering and anointing with sprays, and having drunk a good deal of the wine from the fridge and leaving lots of washing and clearing-up in the kitchen, which took me ages to sort out.

12 February 1987

We have a local cook now for busy patches, Violinda, who is very tranquil, completely unflappable and a superb cook – also a very keen member of the Wednesday night Bible study. A various assortment of people gather around our lovely antique refectory table of an evening in a coming together of different personalities, languages, cultures and interests.

Because of the fine, big, strong, lockable door at the top of the spiral steps, which leads to the flat (our haven of refuge and peace and 'familyness'), the children seem only to have benefitted from the housefuls of guests.

24 December 1987

I cannot recall a more joyous Christmas Eve, from the first glimpse of glorious sunrise through the hall curtains to the late-night laying-down of six bumpy stockings at the ends of various beds – a day of perfect happiness and contentment. I woke before 6.30 a.m., full of anticipation and excitement, and made two dozen mince pies before breakfast, listening to carols while they cooked. I had a special time of prayer, asking for grace, strength, love and joy and to be a blessing to my family and friends amid all the busyness and preparation, not a bear with a sore head to be avoided. And my prayer was answered!

12 April 1988

Spent the weekend with Dona Bemvinda, who helps us with cleaning, and her family. We went to visit some of her relatives in the remoter parts of Monchique and saw the one-roomed cottage where she, her seven brothers and sisters and her parents lived. We drank lovely cold water from the spring above the house, which was the only water supply, and glimpsed a way of life that is rapidly disappearing from these mountain areas, where increasingly young people are drawn away to the coast by the magnet of tourism.

17 March 1989

A group of Portuguese birders phoned last night and will arrive today. It's still a problem reconciling the almost invariably meticulous advance planning of groups from the UK with the spontaneity of our Portuguese friends, who are often unable to say exactly how many and for how long or whether meals will be required or what time the train gets in. We need to be very flexible. This morning as I prepared the bedrooms, though, I was filled with deep satisfaction and joy in our work. What a peaceful, beautiful, simple place it is and what a treat to be able to welcome so many different people to it – knowing they are going to be blessed.

Bob Pullan has been with us for several weeks studying vegetation in the limestone areas. He and Sarah have done lots of work on the flowers, appearing now in their hundreds, and one day last week I joined them on a field trip. We hacked our way through masses of promising scrub and clambered over walls and ditches under the hot sun, and I learnt so much. Bob has a wonderful gift for interpreting the landscape and inexhaustible knowledge of what's what. Streams of incomprehensible Latin names flow from him as we discover new treasures. It was a wonderful day and supper was ready when we got back, which made it even better.

We went to pick up a new assistant warden, Colin Jackson, from the airport yesterday. He arrived with a zipper bag, guitar, fishing rod, baskets, wellies, straw hat and a coat that looked more like another passenger with its bulging pockets – and that was only his hand luggage. His plane was three hours late, so it was 10.30 p.m. by the time we were sitting down to dinner with a group of young birdwatchers and a naturalist from Lisbon. After supper, one of them said brightly, 'And now it is the RIGHT time to look at my slides. There are only a hundred!' They were very good too: birds, flowers, plants, reptiles. Bed at 1.00 a.m.

8 January 1990

I often feel as though my head is only just above water; there has been a dredger at the end of the headland for several weeks to clear a channel for the Alvor fisherman. I feel I need a dredger to clear a channel through our flat sometimes! However, all this may just have something to do with the end of the Christmas holidays. Nearly a dozen of us sat down to most meals for a couple of weeks. Much fun and feasting, laughing, silly games, more feasting and the biggest Christmas tree we've ever had. Our most demanding visitor, without doubt, was Lucy, a three-month-old Bernese Mountain Dog with beautiful orange and white markings all over her exquisitely silky soft black body, huge feet and a huge appetite – she ate through the computer cord on her first night!

Gales, torrential rain and high winds make us wonder if the Algarve we know is the same one the travel agent's brochures enthuse about. Many of our inside walls are varying shades of grey/green/black – in fact, we have an impressive colony of fungi just inside the kitchen. Curtains have nasty black spot mould patches spreading with every deluge, and clothes smell dank and musty in the cupboards. We long for spring so we can air everything out. Yesterday and today the sun has shone – hooray! – and the fine spell looks set to last for a few days.

12 April 1990

We had a simple communion meal together on Good Friday, readings and prayers interspersed with the courses. We covered the tables with white sheets and lots of flowers and candles. It's always a special time, although sometimes I fear I'm too preoccupied with all the practicalities and too tired and too stretched in many directions to be able to enter into it as deeply and meditatively as I'd like.

On the Saturday we all went off and had a marvellous day out on the west coast, cooking *febras de porco* (pork slices) on the clifftop. Then we played games and talked and read on the beach, finally coming home full of fresh sea air and sunshine to a café meal in the village.

Next day, Easter Sunday, communion and worship on the bluffs at the end of the headland at the usual site to greet the sunrise. Breakfast at home was eggs, cereal, fruit juice, coffee, Easter eggs, cards and surprises for everyone.

3 October 1990

As a family we spent four unforgettable weeks with dear friends in Malawi and Kenya over the summer – a time of incredible richness and joy but an experience that also fundamentally challenged our way of life and way of thinking. It has stimulated much discussion and soul-searching about the vexed question of development and how such extensive and desperate poverty should affect our own attitudes and lifestyle. It's a sad and sobering thought that, as we prepare to feast on Christmas turkeys and so on, before too long some of the children and babies we met and held in a Malawian village will be sick or dying for want of enough maize meal to stay alive. The rains failed this year, nearly all the maize bins were three-quarters empty, and the next harvest won't be ready until March.

We've often thought of Portugal as more akin to Africa than the rest of Europe, but on our return it seemed relatively sophisticated and affluent, especially with the opening in July of a huge new shopping complex in Portimão, which we fear will deal a death blow to the family-run stores and supermarkets in the smaller villages, who can't compete with the range of goods or the much lower prices.

However, since getting home at the end of July, there has been very little time to sit quietly ruminating on such things! A constant stream of visitors began to flow through the centre almost immediately, including many wonderful family and friends. We've had people from Portugal, England, Spain, Germany, Holland – old friends, new friends and each coming for different reasons and with different interests and expectations of their time here, but each finding something of the 'fragrance of Christ' and the peace he brings in the middle of life's considerable pressures. One very hot afternoon in August, the Lusitanian Bishop arrived unannounced with his entire family, including Grandpa. Peter was fast asleep after an early morning ringing and had to come round very fast with the help of a lot of cold water.

One of our most memorable occasions during the summer was a whole night spent wader ringing down on the marsh. The entire household came, including nine children and an eight-month-old baby who slept sweetly under the stars in a half-zipped-up suitcase and woke up with a huge smile in the sparkling sunrise.

The autumn ringing programme has been busier than ever and more successful. We've been aware of a strong blessing from God upon it all. It has involved a great deal of hard work and also highly irregular eating and sleeping patterns, but all very worthwhile as the hard information gained adds vital ammunition to the battle for conservation in Portugal.

5 Feb 1991

This month has been a struggle at a personal level, and I've found it hard to make time to read the Bible and pray. I'm apt to wake up with a slight heaviness upon me, a feeling akin to depression; not unlike fear. There are practical reasons for the low mood: post-Christmas fatigue, a succession of minor illnesses, a stiff shoulder and neck, and as the mornings are so cold we all head for the wood burner with cups of tea, homework, odd socks, PE kit et cetera, which doesn't make for deep meditative sessions of prayer. Sometimes I just think I'm not a very good soldier.

Are you still there? It may be more helpful if I wrote a shorter, more concise account without so much detail. But having invited you in, I want very much to try to share honestly the inside track, knowing you won't give up on us, however unimpressive it is.

15 April 1991

It was a lovely time here over Easter, with quite a houseful in the end and lots of uplifting and moving services, including a Good Friday supper reading the account of the Passion, dawn communion on the end of the headland and a big Easter morning celebration in the common room. We arrived back from the student camp on Maundy Thursday. We were responsible for a lovely group of ten students. Two of them gave their lives to Christ during the week, not least because of the quality of love and friendship they encountered at the camp.

Our wonderful cook's daughter was baptised on Easter Saturday, and she invited us to the party on Sunday, the only non-family present at an incredible feast laid on for the clan in a neighbour's garage. There were about forty people, among them a couple whose three-year-old son was killed six months ago in a road accident. Last week, very tragically, their second child, a little girl, was still-born. So many people so desperately need to know about the Lord's great love.

29 May 1991

Very full house lately, including Constantine from Mozambique who is training to be a doctor. He was imprisoned and tortured for three and a half years in his own country for speaking out against the government, and after several years of searching he found the Lord.

The team and family are all well and happy. We are deeply grateful for the closeness and harmony we enjoy and equally deeply aware it's a gift from God and a result of prayer and nothing to do with being easy to live with! I'm sure we're not. But the Lord has given us strong love for each other, and I can honestly say living and working together, as well as being stimulating and creative, is often quite a laugh. I forgive them for all calling me Mum.

We are busy planning leave time back in the UK. The diary is filling up rapidly and we need great wisdom and sensitivity in decision-making. Sometimes people feel wounded if we don't get to see them. *Always* people (especially in supporting churches) know us better than we know them. Sometimes we're thrown when people don't seem to understand what A Rocha is really about, though we sympathise: we are still working on it!

4 November 1991

It's a lovely autumn evening. Thomas Tallis is making beautiful sounds come out of our ancient creaky tape recorder. Bethie is sweetly sleeping and Estie on her way to bed having been curled up on the sofa all evening sketching, with Pippa the puppy snoozing at her feet. Pete is also on the sofa, nodding off in the lovely fire warmth over his Anthony Trollope novel, which he is so much enjoying. We're all feeling very cosy and peaceful.

28 March 1992

The weather has been terrible – weren't Easter holidays ever thus?! But our contentment and joy has been complete as we revel in every single moment God gives us to be a family again, savouring the beautiful closeness with each of the children, reading aloud, playing hilarious card games and hide-and-seek and sardines in the dark and indoor cricket and skittles (using deodorant sticks and assorted Body Shop bottles) and chess and painting and Lego®. In the evening we've been bringing the old round table close to the fire and for our feasts: beef stew and chicken pot roast and seafood rice, with 7Up and Coke and local red wine. Then I give the younger two 'basin baths' as there isn't much water, let alone hot water, and we sit by the fire with books till it's time for bed, when we snuggle down under our duvets, listening to the rain and the wind. Actually, hopeless romantic though I am, honesty compels me to admit that I haven't slept too well, perhaps being extra sensitive to sounds from the children and inevitably overshadowed as we all are by the parting that will be upon us all too soon again. But we are trying to be philosophical and live resolutely in the present, which is proving to be an immense, rich, generous, abundant gift from God.

15 July 1992

Things have been tricky domestically lately. Our cook's daughter has broken her leg and for two weeks she has felt unable to leave her. With a full household it's been difficult to organise at times. Our beloved cleaner handed in her notice two weeks ago, giving up the unequal struggle with a husband who resents her going out to work, even though she loves it and is tearful to have to leave. I've been busy looking for a replacement, who might turn out to be Eva, the baker's wife.

On Wednesday the baker packed his things and left with no warning or explanation. The bakery is closed and looks likely to remain so, certainly for the foreseeable future. The village is alive with gossip and poor Eva is hiding at home, afraid to face people's curious stares.

30 September 1992

God is astonishingly faithful, and somehow the household has held together with its many and varied occupants. Intensive ringing continues all the time and is always a good focal point for visitors. Constant use of two languages, especially in ringing training, is quite tiring, but 1,800 birds have been ringed during the month and we have three young Portuguese students relatively proficient in putting up nets and extracting, processing and logging data.

It is increasingly difficult for us to be off duty even for a moment while on site, with a large team to manage, constant comings and goings, steadily increasing admin and all the lurking pressures of the trust's financial worries. So the only way is to go out or away. Thankfully we were able to take a few days away in the Alentejo in a little pensão overlooking the Guadiana River.

29 January 1993

It has been a very busy week here and I've greatly enjoyed wearing my assorted hats – minding children, visitors, domestic staff and animals while the boss is away! I've been so conscious of the Lord's enabling and help and strength in amazing ways, as always happens when Pete has to go away. Lots of grace for extra demands, especially as I developed quite a nasty cold the day before he left which has made me feel a bit weary from time to time, and I also lost my voice (very good for me!)

Peter's trip to Guinea Bissau went well and he remained fully fit despite opting to eat from the communal dish with the local pastors and their families, which other speakers at the conference declined to do on health grounds. Some of his most helpful conversations took place at these mealtimes.

27 February 1993

Such loving hospitality from Chris and Annie on my flying trip to England. It was especially good to talk together on Wednesday evening. It would be lovely one day for the four of us to have a long evening round the table together, with good food and wine and conversation. So much has happened in all our lives over the last fifteen years or so and we've all done so much changing and learning and growing. Through it all, even the very painful and perplexing times, how faithful and gentle and patient the Father has been. I find it quite exciting and also reassuring to be an unfinished product and to know that God is at work and, more than that, he has promised to finish what he has begun.

THREE

WELCOME

*Small cheer and great welcome
makes a merry feast.*

WILLIAM SHAKESPEARE

Joan of Arc, William Shakespeare, Martin Luther King Jr, Mother Teresa, Queen Elizabeth I, Marco Polo and C. S. Lewis would be high on my fantasy historical dinner party guest list. I'd milk them for stories, advice and book recommendations, probe their motivations and ask them what they'd do differently if they had another shot at life. We'd drink excellent wine and let the candles burn down and everyone would say it was the most memorable night they'd ever experienced.

Who would you invite? Who *do* you invite? In all cultures, meals represent 'boundary markers' between different levels of intimacy and acceptance.[1] A seat at the table is often predicated on expectations of clothing, behaviour and punctuality. Strict unwritten codes maintain a social order, segregating society along economic, generational or cultural lines. This is why it was so radical for Jesus to eat with tax collectors and Sadducees, children and the elderly, priests and prostitutes. In doing so, he was pointing to a new order of things in the kingdom of God in which the greatest would be the least and the least seated in honour at the King's elbow. In one of his most provocative parables, he describes this kingdom as like a wedding banquet given for a king, where guests are sourced from the highways and byways – any old riff-raff that could be found and persuaded to attend. This welcome was *far* wider than the religious establishment of the time was willing to extend. I wonder if things have changed much.

The biblical practice of hospitality goes beyond gathering with our tribe. It might challenge us to open our homes and ourselves to people who are very different from us, who might lack social graces, who take far more than they give, who will never reciprocate or even show gratitude. This kind of hospitality can take us uncomfortably close to our limits, to a place where we become aware of our inadequacies and need both divine and human help to keep graciously giving. Just because it is hard doesn't mean we shouldn't do it. Jesus asks those of us who follow him to take up our cross (Luke 9:23). We need to have a long, hard think before we turn away a guest because of how much it will cost us, in time, energy or cash.

Some of us, though, don't need to be told to push into discomfort. We exceeded our limits miles back and we're coasting on fumes. If that is you, perhaps God would like you to pull into the nearest petrol station and let someone fill up your tank. You might need to be on the receiving end of some TLC for a change, to be reminded of the fact that you look after other people every day of the year and never earn the free gift of grace that is yours regardless.

There is a saying, 'Charity begins at home', which I suggest has an – admittedly less snappy – parallel: 'First be hospitable to your fellow Christians.' Belonging to a church is one of both the best and the worst parts of being a Christian – best because of the people, and worst for the same reason.

I was a student in Birmingham, a city famed for its many curry houses. After the Christian Union on Fridays, a large group of us would often go to one of the cheaper establishments for a balti and naan. On one of these occasions I was at the end of the long table, close enough to overhear someone at the neighbouring table comment to his companions, 'They have to be Christians. Look at them – completely mismatched.' It made me smile. It was true. There were the scruffy arts students, the muscle-bound rugby players, the exhausted medics and the socially awkward mechanics improbably gathered at The Shapla on the Bristol Road. Other than Jesus, there was no explanation for this odd selection of people to have chosen to spend the evening together. As with biological families, so with the family of God. You get who you get, and you have to get on with loving them even if you don't like them very much.

The idea of church members meeting and eating together, sharing resources, celebrating and grieving, is not new. The book of Acts records how early believers 'were together and had everything in common', including property and possessions, and met on a daily basis for worship, prayer and meals (Acts 2:44–7). While some are better at talking about community than living it, you can't avoid the fact the Christian life requires engagement with other Christians.

But how about when it comes to people who don't share our faith, who may indeed openly despise it? Christians bubbled long before the COVID-19 pandemic made bubbling a thing. Christian bubbles form quickly and easily, but they must be popped because they are not how God intended us to live in the world.

There are more people out there than we realise who are not Christians because they have been made to feel like outsiders. The kind of community that God is interested in building doesn't begin by separating people into groups on the basis of what they do or don't believe, but rather by embracing all-comers, equally made in the image of God and loved by him. He has accepted us unconditionally and lavished his forgiveness and love on us. We are not at liberty to offer less.

In A Rocha, as people of many nationalities from many very different cultures have come together because of a common love for the natural world and the commitment to do something practical about its destruction, we have seen over and over again an amazing transformation take place in people's lives as well as in the landscape itself.

In the ecstasy and ignorance of my own conversion experience, and with the sublime confidence of one setting out into an entirely black and white world, I assumed that my wordy proclamations to friends and family (and sometimes people I met on trains) were introducing them to God for the very first time: a completely fresh set of footprints, as it were. I was to learn a lot about God's presence and my own pride in the experience of helping to run the first A Rocha centre for ten years and would begin to detect his footprints and fingerprints everywhere. A whiff of the fragrance of Jesus lurking around someone who has not given his life to Christ? A tender heart showing evident forgiveness while clearly not having received forgiveness herself from the Lord? Increasingly I became aware of a secret history unfolding in every life in which God, acknowledged or not, is the protagonist. Sometimes the very people protesting the loudest spend the most time thinking about him.

We should, of course, not be surprised. Paul makes it shockingly plain in Acts 17 that before we belong to the (wonderful and terrible) community of the redeemed in Christ, we belong even more fundamentally, along with every other man, woman and child, to the community of the created. For 'we are God's offspring', he says (verse 29), and he is referring to all people, including the Greeks and Romans, Jews and Gentiles assembled for the meeting of the Areopagus in Athens, not just to followers of The Way. I started to realise how often I behaved as if this were not the case, treating unbelievers as if they have nothing to offer and everything to receive.

We must go further though; the Gospels make it plain that all Christians are called to welcome fellow believers and those of other faiths or none, yes, but also strangers in need: children removed from damaging parents, traumatised refugees, recovering addicts and newly released prisoners. Not everyone will be involved in welcoming foreign immigrants into our homes – though all of us can look for opportunities to do so – but as the whole body of Christ we can together extend a welcome to everyone who needs one. Whenever we participate in that welcome, the amazing truth is that we are welcoming Jesus himself:

> I was hungry and you gave me something to eat, I was thirsty and you gave me something to drink, I was a stranger and you invited me in, I needed clothes and you clothed me, I was ill and you looked after me, I was in prison and you came to visit me ... Truly I tell you,

whatever you did for one of the least of these brothers and sisters of mine, you did for me.

(Matt. 25:35–6, 40)

One of the paradoxes in life is that sometimes the hardest things we do are also the most rewarding – think climbing large mountains, giving birth, learning complex musical pieces. Extending a welcome to people whose neediness or difference terrifies us can be – let's be honest – very difficult. But it can also be a source of incomparable blessing.

As a family, we invited our friend Hannah to live with us for six months of the coronavirus lockdown during 2020. She has complex and severe mental health struggles, and a long period of isolation could have proved fatal. There were times when her presence confronted me with my own selfishness and shallow, muddy wells of compassion; times when I wanted to block my ears and run away from her pain because hearing about it hurt me too. But most of the time she gave far more than she received from us. She brought puzzles and crafting projects to do with the girls, baked amazing cakes, wrapped me in tight hugs on days I badly missed my mum and poured generous, affirming words over us morning to night. We've all missed her since she moved out.

If you are wondering if this might be a nice anecdote but doubt the principle it illustrates could be replicated in your case, how about you do a little test? Ask God to bring to mind someone who could do with knowing they are not forgotten and alone and see what happens.

EVERYONE, ALL THE TIME?

A few years ago I had what could probably be described as a 'robust conversation' but was actually a rather messy argument with an acquaintance that has continued in my head ever since. Sitting with our flat whites at a wobbly metal table in the back of a cramped London café, we strayed off our official agenda on to one of her passions: the Christian duty to house street sleepers. Perhaps it was because this meeting of ours was my fifth of the day and fifteenth of the week, or maybe because when I would walk wearily through my front door that evening I would be cooking for the ten members of my home group – whatever the reason, I became defensive and cross. It was all very well for her to cram her house with the homeless, I said, but we couldn't all be expected to. You had to have boundaries or you'd burn out. Staring me down, she told me the idea of boundaries was a poor excuse for disobeying God's call to embrace all in need, and that burnout was a fiction invented by the spiritually weak. And I said, 'I know for a fact burnout is real. And I hope God is gracious and doesn't make you learn that the hard way,' meanwhile secretly hoping she would have a very public breakdown within the year. I know: unworthy and horrid. Now you know what I'm really like!

The fact is, she had touched a raw nerve. I live with an undercurrent of fear that when I meet Jesus he might say, 'Who are you? Where were you when I was hungry, cold and alone?' And at the same time, I often misjudge my own capacity, stretching myself to a thin and ragged state where I am of little use to anyone. If you wrestle with the same tension, I hope the following reflections, simple and incomplete as they are, might help.

First, no individual can meet all the needs of the world. My conversation partner had an admirable focus on the dire need for roofs over the heads of those with nowhere to sleep safely. But even with her higher-than-average energy levels and uber-supportive husband, she would have to admit she wasn't doing much for the collapse of biodiversity, the refugee crisis, the increasing numbers of those with depression and anxiety, cancer patients, world hunger or youth unemployment. As the Church we should, can and do address all of the above and more. We are the people of God, the community of the redeemed – one body, not a lot of little independent bodies doing their own thing. God can offer an infinite welcome, but individually we can't. We are finite.

Second, while the Bible challenges us to expand the definition of family, it also honours and acknowledges the importance of marriage and the parenting of children. I've noticed Shawn and I have a tendency to stand side by side or back to back looking out at the world. We're a good team. But if we don't remember to turn and face each other now and then, a feeling of neglect and loneliness creeps in. Our closest relationships can be mistaken for the ones that need the least nurture, but the opposite is true.

Children can be collateral damage in radically hospitable Christian households. A friend of mine who grew up in a Christian conference centre talks about the sense of being parented by everyone and no one and, as an adult, barely speaks to his actual mother and father. Another friend recalls being turfed out of her bedroom over and over again to accommodate the latest short- or long-stay visitor, often finding her stuff moved, broken or gone when she took repossession. Growing up in a full and welcoming home can be a rich and positive experience and certainly doesn't always result in psychological damage, but we do need to be mindful of our children's needs at least as much as – and probably more than – those of others.

We had phases in our family life at Cruzinha when, as children, we were in danger of getting lost in the mêlée. Coming off the school bus in the late afternoon, we'd check who was at home, and often there would be some interesting new arrivals willing to get roped into helping with our homework or drawn into a water fight or board game. The four of us would often target particular individuals to woo into cross-generational friendships, campaigning hard for their inclusion in family outings and holidays until the bloodlines were blurred and indistinct. A door was eventually installed at the top of the winding staircase to our flat, and sometimes the six of us needed to be shut behind it.

There were times when I could tell Mum was hurt by our preference for mixing in with the wider community. And I had times when I resented the number of people who said my mother was like their mother. She had a very big heart, but now and then I wanted more of it for myself. As with most families, we did our best, sometimes making mistakes and needing to forgive each other.

Third, we are all made with different personalities, giftings and preferences. As an extrovert, nothing makes me happier than a noisy houseful (unless I have had a bad night's sleep; tired Jo does not like people being loud). Living in a vicarage a stone's throw from the church in the heart of a friendly and sociable village, we were aware our life here could become an endless series of impromptu tea parties. According to a forthright and bristly elderly gentleman who came to call soon after we moved, the house had always had an open-door policy. As the vicar's family, we needed to be accessible to the community at all times – this was (unbeknown to us) what we had signed up for in being wife and children of the vicar, and he was not a little put out that he could now come by invitation only.

While I like to pack the house, Shawn is an introvert who spends most of his day around people and needs quiet and space to recover. We've needed to compromise and learn that our differences don't represent failings in the other person. I have needed to put his needs ahead of my desire to meet expectations and please people, and he has needed to dig deep and be friendly and sociable more often than he'd choose to be.

To sum up, then: there is no getting away from the fact that being a follower of Jesus means stretching out our arms further than we would expect them to reach. Our guest list is going to be long and colourfully chaotic, and will include not only our friends and family, but also strangers, oddballs and atheists. And in hosting these unlikeliest of invitees, we will discover Christ there in and among them.

COMMUNICATING WELCOME

Once we have decided who is coming, we need to work out how to let them know we want them to feel at home. There are many different rituals used to express welcome around the world. The Masai in Kenya perform the *adamu*, or 'jumping dance', where up to twelve warriors compete to spring the highest into the air. In France, you will be greeted with a kiss on both cheeks, in China with a slight bow, in Ireland with a cup of tea and in Belarus with a loaf of bread and a salt cellar.

As a family, we don't have an official welcome ritual, but we do seem to follow a fairly standard script: 'Hello! So good to see you!' [Insert physical contact as appropriate.] 'We hope you can squeeze into our hovel' [or some other such deprecating humour that acknowledges the outrageous proportions of the vicarage]. 'How was your journey? You found us okay? No need to take off your shoes.' [Or, after a surreptitious inspection reveals mud on said shoes, 'Yes, if you wouldn't mind taking them off that would be great. Whoever thought pale carpets were a good idea?'] 'Make yourselves at home. What can we get you to drink?'

How about you? What is your ritual?

Whether we perform a choreographed dance, string up a banner, slap backs, bear hug or just smile, it is absolutely crucial to get those first moments right. However we say it, our guests need to hear they are wanted and will be provided for. Is there warmth in our voice as we say hello? Does our smile reach our eyes? Does our body language reinforce our words or contradict them, and are we responsive to any sign our guest might be distressed or uncomfortable?

We need to try to anticipate areas of pain and remember that not everybody finds parties easy. It can be hard for unmarried people to be with glowing couples; hard for people in loveless marriages to be with physically demonstrative couples; hard for childless people to see a mother absorbed in a baby; hard for parents of disabled children to see big, happy, carefree families where the children are bright and healthy. The list is endless. We need to exercise sensitivity, develop empathy and be alongside to support, encourage and offer friendship.

And we need to really listen not just to the words, but also to the silences and the feelings underneath the words. A good listener says very little, doesn't offer opinions or draw parallels, and certainly doesn't try to fix it. To 'be there' is one of the greatest gifts we can give.

Chapter 1 of the Gospel of Luke complements the second chapter of the book of Acts by reminding us that even infants in the womb are not excluded from the activity of the Holy Spirit. I have discovered that even children of three or four years of age often have a remarkably uncluttered understanding of what God is up to. With no complicated agendas in the way, they can plough instinctively to the heart of the matter, somehow knowing that people aren't just looking for a hot meal, but for a place to belong.

Several decades ago, one of our friends suffered a severe nervous breakdown and spent many distressing months in a psychiatric hospital. His wife, whose suffering was of course equally intense, somehow embraced this ordeal within the context of her profound faith in a powerful and loving God.

She even eventually thanked him for allowing it because of the new reality that it produced both in their marriage and in her relationship with God, though that was much further down the line. The immediate challenge was how to navigate the transition from the safe, institutionalised routine of hospital to the scary unpredictability of normal life.

The day of his discharge arrived. My heart has always rushed ahead of my mind in decision-making, so I spontaneously called and invited them for family supper that evening. The invitation was gratefully received. As I hung up, panic set in. I had no experience of mental illness and very little clue about how to communicate our genuine concern for someone emerging from such a harrowing experience and venturing for the first time onto the very thin ice of the outside world. However, I sat on my fears, knowing that I could at least prepare my best meal, something appetising and nourishing enough to expel memories of bland hospital fare and rekindle an interest in home cooking. So I set to in the kitchen, burying with busyness the apprehension that floated to the surface every time my brain disengaged from the task. I felt very anxious as they arrived, but the little band of small children drew them in with the usual cheerful friendliness, and soon everyone was seated at the table.

John sat stiffly on one side, his back against the wall, expressionless and silent. Jo, aged four, slipped in beside him, shuffling untidily along the bench until the gap between them disappeared, creating one lumpy form out of two mis-assorted shapes, rather like Pooh and Piglet huddling together on the edge of a rainy Hundred Acre Wood. Simultaneously, she tucked her small hand through his arm and laid her blonde head against his tense shoulder. I realised this wordless gesture communicated more powerfully than anything I could have learnt in a hundred counselling courses the tender, total acceptance he needed in his bewildered fragility. I have myself often experienced the healing balm of childish arms wound around my neck, a small cheek laid trustingly against my own. And countless times I have watched the same miracle take place as unsuspecting visitors received the disproportionate affirmation and comfort of a child's embrace.

Another story. It was a regular evening at Cruzinha, spent with the extended family of Harrises, assistant wardens, volunteers, students and visitors in the common room, talking, laughing and processing the day. Because of the noise, at first no one heard the knock at the door. But eventually, someone did and opened it.

A very tall, very beautiful young Angolan woman stood on the threshold. Leaving the catwalks of Paris and Milan behind her, she had reached the end of the road. Her brother had been to stay before and suggested she come. It wasn't just her tense face but her whole body that expressed dejection and despair. For a split second, we all just looked at her, and then four-year-old Beth rushed forward: 'Don't worry, *we'll* take care of you!'

She became part of the family, and though she couldn't identify moths or flowers or take birds out of nets, we all appreciated her African cooking. She became a Christian, trained as a lawyer and now works in international human rights law.

As God is above and beyond our understanding, metaphors can be our best hope of grasping his infinite, mysterious, divine qualities. We often speak of him as a father, and in doing so we are reaching to capture attributes such as authority, the ability to protect and provide, to teach, guide and correct. But God also embodies the best of what it means to be a mother. I was blessed beyond measure to have a mother who always sounded over the moon to hear my voice on the end of the phone, even if she was rushing out the door or in the middle of a long letter to someone. She threw big celebrations for minor milestones, and even when we were both grown-ups she'd often cry when we said goodbye. So I understand what she meant when she urged us to live in the world with a mother's heart.

God is looking for mothers: both sexes, any age. He is looking for people with that particular quality of totally accepting, generous, self-giving love, who will pour it out extravagantly, like the precious ointment in the Gospel story of Mary's anointing of Jesus, and those who are, or who feel, unloved.

A mother's love is wildly forgiving. 'Love covers over a multitude of sins,' writes the apostle Peter.[2] Motherly love can be so over the top it refuses to see them at all. God's love, on the other hand, sees them clearly and offers enough forgiveness to completely obliterate them.

A mother's love is fierce and protective. God is willing to lay into our enemies when they threaten our safety and even do terrible things to them. The boy who for months terrorised my children on the school bus was shown this aspect of a mother's love in a short encounter neither of us will forget.

God's motherly love for us is always available. There is always a welcome at the throne of grace, and not a ten-minute appointment until we hear a brisk, 'Next, please!' It's an invitation to pour out our hearts before him. He's never in a hurry or distracted or impatient.

No mother ever stops feeling pain for her child, whether she is six months, sixteen or sixty. God will continue to feel our pain until that day when we are whole in his presence. And until then, knowing we are not alone in a pain is the only thing that makes it bearable.

JOANNA'S STORY[3]

You ask me why you have woken to find another stranger in your home, daughter? You seem displeased. Before long you will marry and have your own household and I can see you plan to do things differently. But if you knew Jesus, you would understand. Yes, you were born too late to meet him in body, but believe me, his Spirit is here. I wish you had experienced those years with me. I do.

How to explain the exhilaration and the terror of that time? There were those who followed from a distance, but it was hard to stand apart. You had to choose: with him and for him, or against him, which was safer, no doubt about that. Before long I wasn't counting the cost. My daughter, how I wish you could have been there. Seldom do we women get that close to the action, but we were there alongside the men with Jesus, from beginning to end. I will tell you about a meal. You will see. You will see the effect he had.

You have heard about the miracles, but his teaching was just as powerful. He had a way of taking our Scriptures and turning them so they caught the light. Even the experts paid attention. He asked questions of the Law they couldn't answer. He undermined their authority and it made them fight with each other: they couldn't decide if he was a prophet or a demon. Jesus often taught in the synagogues and public squares. The religious leaders would gather around, shooting their objections like arrows through slitted ramparts.

On this occasion, a Pharisee named Simon made a show of holding a banquet so discussion could continue over food. I suppose he felt he was bestowing a great honour on this Rabbi from the back of beyond. In some regards it was a risk having him in close proximity. By then Jesus had made it clear he had no intention of holding to the purity rituals – he used to say cleanliness was a matter of the heart, not the hands. The Pharisees kept themselves scrubbed and seldom came near anyone whose dirt might rub off on them; Jesus had become filthy according to their reasoning because he associated with the worst of our society's sinners. So perhaps they were doing something brave by eating with him. I am trying to be generous, though they don't deserve it.

They invited him, but then the way they behaved towards him . . . What kind of host makes every effort to dishonour their guest? Yes, I know it was a long time ago. I can't help but raise my voice – it still makes me angry! Not even a kiss at the door. He should have turned on his heel and we'd have all gone with him.

There were many of us in the inner courtyard and it took some time before I was able to squeeze my way into the room where the men reclined around the long, low table. I sensed the tension in the room immediately. Susanna mouthed to me from the opposite corner, 'They didn't wash his feet.' I could feel my cheeks burn, sharing the shame. By craning I could see the soles of Jesus' feet, streaked with the dirt of the road. The servant girls had attended to every other diner as they removed their shoes, but not the Lord's. I would have searched for a basin and towel myself had I not noticed the woman beside me was weeping, trying to dry her face with her sleeve. I reached out to offer comfort, wondering at the cause of sorrow that would show itself in such a setting. But as I did, she slipped through the people in front of us, until she was directly behind Jesus. Her sobs became louder and messier, and though at one end of the table the animated debate continued, a hush grew around her.

The woman was kneeling now, her face low over Jesus' feet so her tears rained over them. Over and over again, she kissed those leathery, dirt-encrusted feet, cradling them gently in her hands. At last, lifting her face, she looked around. No one would give her a towel, so she reached up and released her clasp, allowing her hair to fall scandalously free, using it to mop him dry. We could only look on in horrified fascination as the scene unfolded.

A heady scent hit the back of my nose before I saw what she'd done next. Those closer said afterwards she'd poured an entire jar of perfume over him. Love makes you extravagant. Yes, daughter, your father is an exception. He would not waste a kernel of corn, even on me.

I will go on. There is more to tell. There was no ignoring her presence now. Simon the Pharisee was watching from the end of the table, and you would have thought from his face that the woman had poured out pig urine, not perfume. The town was small: he had seen her around. He knew how she made her living.

Jesus had a masterful way of humbling the proud. It was as though he'd invite them to draw a curtain and they'd find them-selves exposed before they realised what they'd done. Getting Simon's attention, he told a story. There were two debtors, one owing a little, the other an unpayable sum, to the same man. Both debts were written off. Who, he asked Simon, would love this man more? Simon must have seen the trap but couldn't avoid it. 'I suppose the one with the bigger debt.'

'Too right. Do you see this woman?' We all looked, though only Jesus really saw her. 'Where you insulted and demeaned me, she has given me the best she has. This is not her home, but she has made me more welcome than you, Simon. Yes, she has made big mistakes and lived a bad life. That's why she is so full of love for me, who has forgiven her all. You, righteous one, are cold and empty.'

You can understand why they came to hate him, can't you? He saw right through them and played by entirely different rules. Those are the rules we try to live by, daughter. That is why we welcome so many into our home. Do you see now?

A PRAYER ABOUT BEING WELCOMED TO GOD'S TABLE

Big-hearted God, you have set a
table with places for all of us.

You are inviting me to sit and eat and make myself
at home, even though you know my manners are
terrible and I'm liable to grab and gobble.

You are not worried by my neediness.

You will feed me generously, as you will my
fellow diners, until our fear of hunger leaves and
we become satisfied and full of your peace.

Thank you, *thank you* for your welcome.

Amen.

Miranda's journals

1993–1996

31 March 1993

Last night we were invited to the Lagos Rotary Club dinner and Pete was asked to speak and show slides on the Alvor Estuary, the work of the centre and the urgent need to protect the area. He was careful to point out that conservation and tourism don't necessarily conflict, and that an increasing number of visitors are in search of the wildlife and natural beauty of the Algarve, not just its beaches and cheap wine. Many influential businessmen and people in local government were there, the talk was well received with some good discussion, and they plan to visit Cruzinha soon. It was a bit like a church service without Christ; instead of grace at the beginning of the meal there were various little speeches and a sort of flag-holding ceremony. The image of Peter semi-draped in a large national flag will stay with me for a long time, and I'm very glad Jo wasn't there to give me an uncontrollable fit of the giggles.

1 April 1993

It's wonderful having the family home from school, yet the days when school holidays and continuing centre life coincide are rather like a circus act with a lot of juggling of priorities and always the fear of dropping an important ball. Yesterday, for example, we had forty local schoolchildren watching the ringing, helping unload the moth trap and learning about frogs ... the fourth such school visit in a week. Then some students on motorbikes arrived from Faro, eager to train as ringers; they will start next week. In the afternoon, four British visitors arrived for tea just as I was leaving to take Beth to ballet and Peter was off to play tennis with the others.

We have a volunteer here at the moment, sent to us by a local bishop after a few days trying to help him. He has run away from England to try to escape his problems, which are many and deep, and he has given us a few hair-raising moments, though he seems to have responded reasonably well to the experience of family life and some TLC.

30 May 1993

There have been three suicides in the immediate area this last week. One of them was a married lady with two grandsons. Another was an elderly man who jumped from a fifth-floor balcony. Miguel, who works at Cruzinha and is his neighbour, tried to restrain him and was left with his coat in his hand. He has been very shaken by it. There was also a murder last week – someone finally shot his old enemy. The villagers say he was a bad man and deserved to die. Behind the passive, resigned faces, many people exist in a state of quiet desperation – they need a saviour and a deliverer. We pray on for this outwardly calm and peaceful yet inwardly turbulent area.

10 June 1993

We've had a whole variety of visitors here lately, ranging from the Wash Wader Group who came for two weeks last month to some watercolour artists on a painting holiday, and this morning three young American musicians from the Seville Philharmonic Orchestra will leave after a short visit. One is a Mormon, one a recent Christian convert and the third a cheerful atheist. Two of our

Portuguese trustees are here for a few days still. The effect that Cruzinha seems to have on the people who visit never ceases to amaze us – opportunities for ministry and witness arise all the time, and we feel very privileged as people open up and begin to share their real feelings and needs.

In the house at the moment we have Phil, who is painfully finding his way back to Christian things and needs a bit of unscrambling – a very dear guy; Wim, a Dutch teacher recovering from some kind of nervous breakdown; and Jane, an old friend who became a Christian a few years ago but hasn't, I think, really taken off in her faith yet. There continue to be many opportunities for talking, listening, praying and counselling, and we constantly need to pray for wisdom, discernment and love.

In the village too there is a continuing sense of God at work, even though progress is painfully slow. After years of carefully explaining the gospel, many people remain deeply confused; there seems to be widespread spiritual blindness and deafness.

3 September 1993

Long walk this morning with a volunteer who has deep and difficult problems in her life, mostly about motherhood but also wanting to go on with God but being paralysed with fear. I pray the Holy Spirit would gently fill her like healing, soothing oil, trickling into all the dry, hurting places, and also that Jesus would lead her from her place standing by the door, wanting to bolt, right onto the Father's lap, with his arms enfolding her in a strong, warm embrace. Those two images remain with me. I'd like to pray very honestly that the Lord will meet with her and with them all very powerfully in his own time and his own special way.

11 November 1993

Today is Saint Martin's Day and tonight, after *arroz de pato* (duck rice), the house will fill up with local friends and neighbours coming in to celebrate with figs, roasted chestnuts, port, wine and the season's first mince pies – these last not an ancient Portuguese custom! We've invited all and sundry and hope very much lots of people will come.

It has been an encouraging few weeks at Cruzinha on all fronts. Despite unpredictable and at times very stormy weather, the ringing has been intensive and very useful, with some real highlights, including five azure-winged magpies Saturday lunchtime. There are only two populations of these rare and beautiful birds in the world, one here and one in China, and for a time we had thirty-six of them roosting in the pines below the house.

I've taken over the moth studies from Adrian Gardiner and Pete Sturgess and definitely risk getting hooked. It's very exciting to unload the trap each morning and attempt accurate identification with the limited resources available.

Both these activities continue to be a focus for residents and casual visitors, also teachers, students, ornithologists, naturalists and casual dropper-inners. We've had some excellent times with visitors and many signs of God at work, not least in the planning and timing of when people come and who else is here at the time.

We've had excellent team times too – everyone is tired, but not ragged, and recently we've had several 'just us' evenings, with big feasts and time to talk and laugh and play silly games and relax together.

8 March 1994

Sometimes the pressure has been very acute recently, but we are learning to experience the truth that 'all things work together for good for those who love God, who are called according to his purpose'.[1] I personally am learning to welcome even the dark and difficult times as strange harbingers of God's grace and love. They seem to be times of learning and growth. Much of the time I feel well out of my depth with all that is going on in the various departments of our life, so it's a question of either walking on the water or sinking completely. I praise God daily for himself, a wonderful family, faithful friends, a magnificent team, the challenging and satisfying work and the fact that the future belongs to him too. He has set our feet upon a rock and therefore we are secure. What a privilege.

A picture is just beginning to emerge of our post-Portugal future – perhaps an emphasis on training and vision-sharing, especially in the Global South but anchored in practical, local, conservation work, possibly in France. We are anxious not to run ahead of the Lord in all this and to wait until he gives us a clear green light.

25 April 1994

We had a wonderful houseful over Easter – twenty-two of us sat down to a special Good Friday supper incorporating communion and the reading of the Gospel up to the crucifixion, some praying and the singing of hymns. Someone also had a birthday, so we had a birthday cake and sang happy birthday somewhere in the middle, which funnily enough didn't seem too incongruous.

Easter morning at sunrise found us all at the end of the headland for communion, worship and praise to the Risen Son in the rising sun! Followed by a distinctly chocolatey breakfast. Then later I cooked half a lamb and all the trimmings for a very festive lunch. Another family came over for tea. My first ever attempt at a simnel cake was okay, I think. By the time the latest visitor had arrived at about 8.00 p.m. and we had all had a late supper, we were all rather full and tired.

31 May 1994

'My time at Cruzinha was so good for me and has really set me back on the right track. My relationship with the Lord has definitely taken an upward turn and I feel able to persevere as a Christian working in the environmental field.' Letters like that are hugely encouraging to us all here as we attempt to demonstrate the coherence of a life corporately and actively lived in the presence of God in all the multiplicity of goings-on that make up a typical week. Several people have written following their time here to say they have started talking with God again. It's such a privilege to witness time and again his gentle activity in people's lives.

The whole process of selecting and appointing the new wardens was immensely draining all round and a huge relief when the decision was finally made. Now we are trying to make sure that everything is in good order for the handover. A major drains problem surfaced last week and the sins of the original builder found him out, involving him in a complicated and very smelly replumbing exercise, which was embarrassing with a house full of visitors, including one or two very little ones. Everyone was remarkably tolerant and philosophical, and we all survived the upheaval.

We have had a lot of visitors in a seamless succession of arrivals and departures. It is sometimes a little dizzying, and always interesting, stimulating and challenging. My greatest worry is that of running out of personal resources in terms of genuine, welcoming love and the capacity to be involved in double listening: what is this person saying? And what is God wanting to say to this person? We depend very heavily on the Lord for the energy and strength to keep going out to people, to keep being available to look after them properly and to find the best ways of involving each one in what is going on. Smaller children always love to 'fly the birds' after they've been ringed. Bigger visitors enjoy that too. Being so closely involved with the raw material of creation is always a profoundly moving experience and often a source of healing too.

1 June 1994

Yesterday a Cornish/German couple arrived with teenagers Apollo and Zion, saying that the Lord told them to come to us. They had no petrol, no money or food, but were entirely confident he would meet their needs — which he did, abundantly, through Violinda's lamb and roast potatoes!

28 August 1994

Yesterday a group of Portuguese people from the north arrived at 9.00 a.m., having travelled overnight, and the outgoing people were still asleep. Twelve of us had slept out on the beach that night to watch some especially good shooting stars and overtook the arriving group in the lane on our way home. It was a question of taking a deep breath, making strong coffee and setting to making beds, shifting rucksacks, cleaning bathrooms and so on.

There has been yet another setback in the saga of a reserve on the Alvor Estuary. Despite the recent encouragements as the process to create the Protected Area goes forward, there have been signs that the developers and the local council are trying to create loopholes in the law in order to allow construction of a marina and major tourist infrastructure. A Rocha has been busy campaigning against what would be the irreversible destruction of vital habitat on and around the Estuary. We are praying that environmental good sense will prevail over the ancient desire for a quick buck, and for all the team in the often-discouraging moments during the campaign.

4 September 1994

Life lately has been hectic, as usual, but we are becoming familiar with the Cruzinha juggling act – constantly changing housefuls of students and visitors of various nationalities, lots of day visitors, a full ringing programme, renewed pressure from developers, plumbing problems and unexpected arrivals: two puppies, a guinea pig and a hoopoe with a badly broken wing all on the same day recently. Sometimes, as I've sat down to lunch under the rubber tree with twenty or so others, I've been tempted to contemplate the relative attractions of a slightly smaller family! But no, it's a brilliant life, and what a privilege to be doing this and how exciting to watch God at work in little and sometimes bigger ways. Though we sometimes feel we are running out of steam, we never actually do. Hooray for siestas, which are a great idea on stuffy, sultry days when getting from A to B feels like moving concrete blocks.

17 January 1995

We had a wonderful Christmas and New Year. We had expected some sad moments, this being one of the more major 'last times' and Cruzinha Christmases having become something of an institution, but in fact it was the best ever, I think, and apart from the odd occasion helping one or other of the children come to terms with leaving this dearly loved home, we all enjoyed the festivities to the full. We had a massive, long-needled pine tree, lots of over-the-top decorations, a 12kg turkey and all the usual occasions with friends and neighbours. Penny and I took the usual twenty-five or so plates of goodies around the village on Christmas Eve and I made something over fourteen dozen mince pies, all of which disappeared as if by some conjuring trick almost the minute they came out of the oven.

24 February 1995

We are approaching what amounts to a relaunch of A Rocha on a more international scale. Not surprisingly, there is some pressure associated with it, but there are exciting days with requests for help coming in quite literally from all over the world – Argentina, Peru, Poland, India and South Africa. We have invitations to teach in Canada and the States and elsewhere. All the literature is being radically changed and updated and an A Rocha office has been set up in the UK. The next few months will be critical as we see whether we can raise financial backing for all these opportunities.

18 March 1995

Dates are now fixed and we leave Cruzinha on 22 June. Portugal has been home for twelve years, and uprooting is a painful process all round. We've been at full stretch for a while, trying to leave everything in good order for the new leaders and at the same time doing a lot of forward planning and praying. Meanwhile, visitors continue to pour through Cruzinha – twenty-two to feed and water this week.

As I've begun preliminary cleaning-up jobs, sorting the more jungly cupboards and corners in the flat, I've sometimes felt God is doing his own spring-clean in me. I am determined to know God and trust him and experience the reality of the promise in Philippians 4:9, the guaranteed personal presence of the God of peace himself.

18 April 1995

The Dutchman and his Portuguese girlfriend who live on the land adjacent to Cruzinha have illegally installed two vast caravans and a generator on the back of a lorry, and they see it as a long-term arrangement. As well as being unsightly, it causes serious disturbances to the ringing, and we've asked for an assurance that they will move soon, or the police will become involved. Their long-term plan is to build there (also illegal), which would be disastrous. This is a tricky situation, not least as the man is an unpleasant person to deal with. It requires wisdom, diplomacy and much prayer. We are often disturbed until 5.30 a.m. by incredibly loud music.

2 August 1995

The last few months in Portugal flew by in the flurry of sorting, packing, preparing for the handover and far too many enormous meals in the process of saying farewell to many very dear friends. Over it all, despite the tears, was a strong sense of God's peace, a task completed, the right moment to move on, and profound gratitude to the Lord for his amazing faithfulness over these years.

1 September 1995

The weeks in Zimbabwe with Alan were incredibly rich for us as a family. He provided a safe context in which to 'be' – to talk, pray, laugh, do and see things together and help each other through the odd moment of feeling homesick or rootless or unsettled.

These few days before term starts are always the hardest of the year for me, and with Beth starting too, I have lost my buffer zone completely. Of course, we knew it wouldn't be easy at this point, with no home base from which to organise for returns to school as well as our own mobile life. Gauntlet Removals added to the complexity of the situation by delivering the wrong boxes to Somerset yesterday. We had arranged for various books, files and winter clothes to be stored with our friends here, accessible until we leave for Canada in January. They then rang later in the day to say they were unable to trace the rest of the contents of our home. I did a quick run through and decided that, with all the children safely under the same roof, the rest didn't matter too much, although I would be sad about the photo albums and my grandmother's chest. Yet another phone call clarified that the load is still in Portugal and not at the bottom of the sea and will eventually reach the depot in Liphook, hopefully in time for me to retrieve the Christmas cake.

Peter is doing an excellent job of staying on top of admin, borrowing phones, computers and kitchen tables and preparing sermons and meetings in lots of improbable places. It is challenging trying to work out our changing roles in this new phase. I am scared but also excited.

4 March 1996

Four months ago we were in Argentina; now I am writing looking out over the Pacific from Galiano Island on the other side of the world in Canada. We have taken responsibility for two courses at Regent College and are living in the home of a couple who are away on sabbatical, sharing it with their adult son, and periodically groups of students – very Cruzinha-like.

The wood-built house is surrounded by forests and full of flowers. Bald eagles are everywhere, the ducks bobbing in the bay and sitting on the rocks in the stream beside the house include harlequins, bufflehead and hooded mergansers. We haven't come face to face with a bear yet.

The family is virtually self-sufficient in regard to food; the large pantry is stocked with preserves, and strings of garlic, onions, wrinkly red chillies and peppers hang from the beams in the kitchen. There is no garbage disposal system – almost everything is recycled or reused.

9 May 1996

How amazing to be in England in May! Thanks to medication, the runny nose and itchy eyes are under control and I'm now revelling in the glories of early summer in Hertfordshire, especially around All Nations, with its carpets of bluebells and daffodils, tall copper beeches mingling with countless pale greens and yellows. There are baby rabbits, pheasants and partridges just everywhere. I think they take divine protection for granted — they're so sublimely confident you have to be careful not to walk on them! We are grateful to find ourselves in such a remarkable community of international and cross-cultural Christian people again. It's a real privilege to meet, talk and pray with these interesting and lovely people.

We are living in a little flat at the top of the main building and enjoying having a place to invite people for port and cheese, muffins, pancakes and maple syrup, hazelnut coffee or whatever.

16 June 1996

Convalescing after surgery with Annie and Chris, and I can't begin to describe how restful and safe it felt to be with them. Annie had thought of so many loving and thoughtful touches, from prunes to freesias to endless beverages and overflowing fruit bowls and a whole succession of mouth-watering meals. The bed was soft and there were sounds of music, talk and laughter in the house all day. Her Spirit-filled company was an extraordinary gift – all the wisdom and comfort and laughter she poured out and the fact that although she is so busy with a thousand and one calls on her time and energy, she never appeared rushed and always had time to be present.

14 August 1996

My main focus this summer [at Au Sable Institute of Environmental Studies, Michigan] has been on the family and hospitality. Lots of people have come for meals, including one evening where, with some help, I cooked an Iberian meal for all seventy-five Au Sable residents.

I have also done a series of short meditations for the board meeting using Jeremiah 17:7–8 and choosing roots by the water as a theme. The prolonged uprootedness and extreme uncertainty of the future are taking their toll and I'm experiencing a familiar dread about goodbyes to the family as the new term comes over the horizon. All four are amazing and a constant source of comfort and consolation.

Jo is on good form and she and Estie have worked hard this summer doing odd jobs around Au Sable. She is looking forward to starting work as an au pair in London before heading to Zimbabwe in December. We are praying she finds her own ways of staying rooted, establishing patterns of prayer and worship and so on to keep her bearings in the new wide open and unprotected world she's about to be launched into. She is a bit apt to fly by the seat of her pants, but maybe that's okay?!

FOUR

AT THE TABLE

Eat, drink and be glad.

ECCLESIASTES 8:15

A salad of grains, bright pomegranate seeds, tart salty feta and mint from the garden. A whole roast chicken, crispy skin bursting to release steaming hot herb-infused juices. Red peppers, skin blackened and flesh sweetened, drizzled in peppery olive oil and speckled with herbes de Provence. A loaf pulled floury and fragrant from the oven, awaiting only a crowning slab of salty yellow butter. Watermelon: the taste of summer. Cake, dense with grated carrot, plump raisins, pecan nuts and pineapple and smothered with cream cheese icing. Nectarines served with tangy Greek yogurt, lavender honey and toasted almond flakes. Home-made elderflower cordial, coffee and frothy milk, a crisp white wine on a hot day. These are a few of my favourite things. I love eating and drinking them and I love making them for people.

There are many reasons why hospitality the world over revolves around food, which we will consider together, once you have made yourself a snack. Writing that paragraph made me hungry, so it is possible reading it had the same effect. We will think about what we communicate in our choice of menu, how food is both a beautiful gift and a source of pain, and the place of shared meals in forming relationships.

Whether the kitchen is your happy place or the least frequented corner of your house; whether you hate cooking or love it so much you sleep-talk about your beautiful Japanese steel cleaver; whether you have a state-of-the-art stove or only a microwave, we can all feed people. We can feed them and we can invite them into a community of belonging. This is something we can all do, as I learnt from a dear friend called Betty who belonged to our church when Alexa and Charis were tiny.

Betty helped in the crèche every Sunday and often babysat for us, arriving rather puffed on her bicycle and invariably bearing carefully chosen toys and activities to keep the girls entertained. On their birthdays she would take us all to Bekonscot Model Village and Railway, or somewhere else we couldn't afford to go unless someone treated us. She often joined us for meals and family outings, but until shortly before she retired and moved away to live with her brother, we were never invited to her home. All we knew was that it was somewhere on the grounds of the school where she had worked with the youngest ages for many years.

When the first and last invitation came, we met her at the prearranged time at the school gates. She led us through the playground and into a block of classrooms, along some gloomy corridors and up two flights of stairs until we came to a floor which seemed dedicated to storing broken school furniture and extra cleaning supplies. She finally stopped at an unpromising looking door and pulled a key out of her pocket. We stood silently for a moment, taking in a poky little room into which was crammed a single bed, a chest of drawers, an armchair and a ceiling-high pile of large Tupperware boxes. On a table in the far corner was a microwave with a stack of plates, mugs and cutlery balanced precariously on top, a kettle on the floor beside it: this was the extent of her kitchen. On every available space on the walls were hung framed photos, among them a picture of the girls she had taken in the park the previous summer. This was Betty's home of almost two decades.

The four of us perched in a row on her bed and, as a magician might pull rabbit after rabbit from an empty top hat, she produced a feast that made the girls' eyes shiny and wide: iced buns, apple slices, packets of crisps, mini sausages, cold pizza and cherry tomatoes. The food kept coming – far more than we could ever eat. She moved a laundry basket off the chair and sat beaming with satisfaction at the success of the event.

It was one of the most moving and generous acts of hospitality I have ever experienced. I can only imagine the courage it must have taken to reveal the humble reality of her life to us. I will never forget it. When we left, Betty gave the girls big hugs and said she hoped we would stay in touch, which I'm happy to say we did until she died several years later.

Community is a complicated word. Like one of those huge lorries that thunders past on the motorway, it isn't always obvious what's in it. It's an emotive term which may awaken longing, panic or just mild curiosity. As one of A Rocha's core commitments, we have tried to define what it means to us, and why we regard it as central to our organisational identity, while at the same time recognising that there are an almost infinite number of creative ways of expressing it. So why is it so important? And why was John Stott so good at it on so many different levels?[1]

First, it matters because, like church, it is a 'given', a fact, not something we can opt in or out of, depending on how much time is left over when work and family obligations have been fulfilled, or a kind of hobby to dabble in at weekends. Christians have always understood community better than most. The one true God whom we worship has his being in three equal and interdependent parts, Father, Son and Holy Spirit. The early church functioned as an interdependent body, sharing all things in common. Building community in our own day requires more intentionality, since we belong to a society that is undeniably and unashamedly committed to individualism (and a whole lot of other -isms which don't belong here).

As a single person, an exceptional leader and one who travelled often and far, John might well have sidestepped this awkward aspect of discipleship. His personality, family background and education did not necessarily equip him well for close personal relationships. In his early days as Rector of All Souls Langham Place, he was known to be particularly cautious in his relationships with the admiring women in his congregation, whom he sometimes referred to as the Langham Ladies – one of whom, at least once, got to lovingly iron his surplice! In later years I think he increasingly allowed himself to be built into numerous communities as a family member, beloved by children and adults alike. One might say he joined the small community of our own family one hot June day in 1985. Dashing through the front door of our rented Portuguese house, desperately trying to avoid some looming crisis in the kitchen, I thrust our three-week-old baby into the arms of a white-haired stranger in a light blue suit, standing in the shadowy hallway. Returning a few moments later I found John gently rocking her, tutting in a soothing way, and we introduced ourselves. Thus began twenty-five years of friendship with our family. Such stories are multiplied hundreds of times over around the world.

I should add that his singleness was no obstacle to giving generous hospitality as well as receiving it, even though the crucial role of his remarkable secretary and friend Frances Whitehead in actually getting food and drink to the table must be gratefully acknowledged! Whether at the Rectory in the early days of his ministry at All Souls – which, incidentally, he shared with a succession of students and others – or later in his tiny flat in Bridford Mews, countless people were warmly welcomed into his home.

There was a playfulness to John, not often seen in public, but familiar to his family and many friends. The Hookses in Pembrokeshire was the setting for innumerable gatherings and became a sort of community in its own right, over which John presided with equal measures of focused work and determined relaxation. Days were spent laying concrete paths, building bird hides, clearing drains or dredging the pond. Evenings were frequently passed reading out loud, often the stories of Saki, which John found hilarious. One visitor was gently rebuked for not laughing loudly enough and encouraged to let his hair down! Back in London, Frances Whitehead, along with a series of gifted young study assistants, became the steadiest and most permanent of all the communities to which John belonged, referred to at any one time as 'The Happy Triumvirate.'

John was unambiguous about the Christian's responsibility to belong to a church. His own life-long local church community was All Souls, and his commitment and loyalty to it never wavered through the years. In fact, even as a schoolboy at Rugby, a leader at many Christian camps and later as a

Cambridge undergraduate, he took his commitment to building Christian community extremely seriously, convening endless tea parties. These often turned into ongoing groups, usually for discussion and study, encouraging young people to integrate faith with complex contemporary issues by engaging in what he called 'double listening' – to the voice of Christ and to the voice of culture. In this way, many small communities came into being. As with everything else he undertook, however, these initiatives were never casual or merely social, but intentional and purposive.

Involvement in the global church community occupied an increasing amount of John's time and energy. He was passionately committed to unity based on biblical truth, wherever possible trying to bridge theological and ecclesiastical divides by means of careful listening, rigorous study and vigorous debate. He was unusual in first challenging his opponents face to face, never in conversation with others, or in print. And in his lifelong endeavour to earth good theology in godly lifestyles, he consistently applied his academic research to his own life and relationships, as well as expecting others to do the same.

Latterly, St Barnabas College became the community that John embraced and belonged to right up to the final days of his life. True to character, he treated everyone there, however humble their role, with equal appreciation and courtesy, even in times of great weakness and pain, his amazing memory for names only failing him at the very end.

Of course, John had his eye always on the only truly permanent community, of which all these others are merely a foretaste, for, like Abraham, 'he was looking forward to the city with foundations, whose architect and builder is God' (Heb. 11:10).

SOUL FOOD

Have you ever noticed the central role of food in the sweep of the biblical narrative? God's gift to Adam and Eve: a largely edible creation. Forbidden fruit: the ostensible reason for the Fall. The curse: the grind of crop cultivation. A famine taking Joseph to Egypt to become a great people; manna in the desert sustaining them in newly found freedom from slavery; food laws cementing their cultural identity; a promised land, flowing with milk and honey. It is no wonder so many of the stories about Jesus take place around meals.

What we experience around the table is far more than the satisfaction of our biological requirements. Eating is about belonging and spirituality, identity and culture and our connectedness to the rest of the created world. As convenor and cook, therefore, you are also an orchestral conductor, circus ringmaster, air-traffic controller, experimental chemist and simultaneous translator. Watch as, around your table, food does its magic – easing tension, soothing anxiety, bringing comfort, delight and renewed energy. The physiological process of digestion is itself designed to relax taut muscles, and certain foods reduce cortisol and adrenaline, the hormones that drive our fight or flight responses.

The location of the eyes of most of the animal kingdom mean they either look down at their food while they eat or out to the side to watch for predators. Humans can eat face to face, maintaining eye contact through a meal.[2] There's a reason why high-level business deals get thrashed out over dinner and why diplomats spend a lot of their lives eating and socialising ('You are spoiling us, Mr Ambassador, with these Ferrero Rocher!').

Mealtimes are a reminder of the rhythm of work and rest God established when he made the universe. Times of toil are necessarily interspersed with replenishment and festivity: 'Life is not only travail and labour, it is also refreshment and joy in the goodness of God. We labour, but God nourishes and sustains us. And this is the reason for celebrating,' wrote Dietrich Bonhoeffer in his seminal work on community, *Life Together*.[3]

If you are an astronaut surviving on reconstituted powders or on a restricted diet for a medical reason, you might not immediately see the connection between eating and celebrating. But God has ordained in his great wisdom and goodness that eating, and especially eating in company, should be one of the most profound and pleasurable aspects of being human. 'Eat your food with gladness,' says Ecclesiastes 9:7; 'Eat what is good, and you will delight in the richest of fare,' urges Isaiah 55:2. Jesus enjoyed dinner parties so much he was accused of being a drunkard and a glutton. That God sweetened a daily necessity by imbuing it with creativity, beauty, discovery and challenge offers us enormous insight into his nature: food is nothing less than an opportunity for encounter with our Creator.

It is possible to leach all pleasure from food consumption – I watched my brother do it during a period of his youth largely devoted to the creation of muscle mass. At set times of the day, he would wolf down unholy numbers of eggs, tins of tuna, pans of plain pasta and, horror of horrors, protein shakes, converting this staggering intake into sinewy lumps and bumps over his upper body. Bodybuilders are willing to make sacrifices towards their (from my perspective) peculiar goal, but we are mistaken if we think there is anything godly about repressing our enjoyment of delicious food.

Babette's Feast is the tale of two elderly sisters who live in a remote part of coastal Denmark in the nineteenth century.[4] Their father, a pietist Protestant pastor, had opposed their respective prospects for marriage: a Swedish cavalry officer and a Parisian opera singer. As obedient daughters, they therefore remained single, eventually outliving him to preside over an austere and ageing sect.

One day a woman knocked on the door, seeking refuge with the sisters, at the opera singer's recommendation, from counter-revolutionary bloodshed in Paris. She served for fourteen long years as their cook and housekeeper for room and board. Each year, she bought a lottery ticket. When a ticket finally won her a huge sum of money, instead of using it to leave Jutland and begin a new life, she invited the sisters and key members of the community to a meal as an expression of her gratitude.

Throughout the days preceding the event, increasingly exotic ingredients began to arrive: a live turtle, quails, truffles, caviar, foie gras and a vast array of wines to pair with each dish. Fine china, crystal and silverware were delivered, and yet more food. It turned out Babette had been a celebrated chef.

As she disappeared into a whirlwind of preparation, conster-nation grew among the prospective diners, who debated how they should handle all this terrifying excess. Theirs was a spiritu-ality devoid of colour and life and they felt themselves being dragged towards a sinful lapse of control. Feeling trapped, as they believed Babette should be permitted to express her grati-tude to them, they decided they would eat the food but in such a way that it left no impression on their palettes.

The evening came, and to begin with the plan seemed to be working. But the artistry of Babette's cooking, the quality and variety of the dishes, the candlelight and the wine slowly broke down the barriers to joy they had carefully constructed over decades. This wholehearted and costly gift had achieved nothing short of spiritual redemption for a community that had forgotten how to live lovingly and wholeheartedly.

WHAT'S FOR DINNER?
In 2016, a British chef set himself the challenge of recreating Babette's feast, but to my knowledge it hasn't been done before or since, and I'm not even sure a meal that lavish *should* exist outside the pages of a novel. Turtle and foie gras are ethically

problematic on their own. So let's say we're off the hook for throwing a dinner that would cost us our life savings. How do we decide what to serve up?

The author and journalist Michael Pollan makes the case that in the Global North, food has come to be viewed with fear and suspicion, put under a microscope and labelled by component. Instead of a punnet of blueberries, antioxidants; smoked mackerel, omega 3; custard tart – ALERT! ALERT! Back away from the cholesterol! Most food packaging is only intelligible to a chemistry graduate. Apparently, we are happy to put a combination of twenty unrecognisable substances into our bodies so long as they are low in fat and sugar. Taste doesn't even come into it.

Deciding what to serve up for dinner could easily become a migraine-inducing gauntlet of complex mathematical problems to solve, but good news! Pollan has distilled all we need to know into three guidelines: Eat food. Not too much. Mostly plants.[5] As with all good gifts, food can be perverted in numerous ways, whether treating it as fuel, foe or god. Our challenge and privilege is to persevere in receiving food as the gift it is and to share it joyfully and generously with others.

My friend Mo takes cookbooks to bed and falls asleep planning menus. For the gastronomes among us, putting together a feast for friends is one of life's greatest pleasures. There are definitely occasions that call for a banquet, not a tin of beans: the return of a prodigal son a prime example. Or a graduation, new job, engagement, retirement or anniversary. If you like feasting you can usually find an excuse: the cat's birthday, one hundred years since the invention of the toaster, someone somewhere getting a particularly flattering haircut – light up the barbeque and season the steaks!

Yet good hospitality has nothing to do with rich, complex or exotic food, so if you don't even have a cookbook to take to bed with you, fear not. A packet of digestives, an apple or a bag of oats might do the job as well as anything more complicated or better.

While a student in Vancouver in my early twenties, I was slogging through one of my fairly regular patches of depression. One morning I awoke feeling like I had reached bedrock. I could not imagine there being anywhere deeper or lower to go, and, to add to the misery, I had three essay deadlines the next day, it was raining and there was no food in the house. Fortunately, I had a lifeline. My friend Kate came over, scooped up me and all my books and piles of paper and sat me on her sofa while she made me a bowl of porridge with brown sugar. I can remember the taste of it to this day. It tasted like hope. I stayed with her for a week and began to float back up to the surface. This is very similar to how God brought Elijah out of his death spiral following his dramatic showdown with the prophets of Baal – letting him get some deep sleep, providing him with fresh bread and water and sending him someone to keep him company (1 Kings 19:4–14).

Porridge and bread – about as basic as you can get, but simple food is all that is needed in almost every situation. Most of the world, for most of history, has had no other choice. Jesus would have had a very limited diet of rough, gritty barley bread, beans, eggs, salted fish, figs and honey. Meat was a rare treat and most fruit and vegetables were largely inaccessible other than the occasional cabbage or leek. We who are privileged to be able to procure ingredients to whip up whatever we happen to fancy may do well to pause and remember now and then that this is not normal or even necessary.

There are ways to spice up even frugal fare, though. I've always enjoyed being served stories with my food: 'This pasta dish was the first thing I ever cooked, and it convinced my now wife to go on a third date.' 'When I was at university, I put vodka into nearly everything I made and got people to try and guess the secret ingredient.' 'My grandmother was given this recipe by her grandmother and I always thought it was unique to our family until I realised it was basically your standard Spanish omelette.' Food can be a gateway into a deeper understanding of another person's history – the flavours, techniques and symbolism that formed them. Perhaps that's why eating in the neutral territory of cafés and restaurants has become so popular in societies where individualism and privacy are prized.

As with all aspects of hospitality, the dishes we serve can be love on a plate or as toxic as takeaway left out overnight. The difference is made by the degree to which we are genuinely seeking to care for others. Sometimes this is simply a matter of figuring out what is likely to be familiar for our guests. We may be adventurous eaters, but a bucket of snails and a side of sheep's brain is likely to be a bit daunting to most people around your table because it will be new, and new, when it comes to food, is risky. We're wired to be cautious of novelty for very good reason – it would otherwise be all to easy to kill ourselves by eating interesting-looking mushrooms and berries. Allergies and intolerances pose genuine risks, and thoughtlessness on our part could have drastic consequences. No one wants to make a fuss or come across as a picky eater. If they've let us know they can't eat peanuts or gluten or lactose or shellfish, they need us to take heed. Allowing us to put food on their plate is an act of trust.

Preference is slightly different, but unless we're cooking for our own small children, the kind thing is to take taste into account. When I first brought Shawn home for Christmas, he gamely tried each new traditional seasonal treat offered to him. Mince pies, Christmas cake, Christmas pudding – Mum produced each one with new hope it would meet with his approval. Three Christmases later, she had come to accept that as he didn't like dried fruit, the chances of him liking confectionery consisting chiefly of dried fruit were slim to none. With his addition to the family came a new Christmas tradition: pecan pie. The rest of us had to continue to pretend we liked mince pies, but his struggles were over, at least.

After the first time I stayed with Shawn's aunt and uncle, Scott and Debbie, in Minneapolis, the house would be stocked with everything I said I liked on the visit before, and I have never had to use my own teabags in their home, which for an Englishwoman abroad is an unusual situation! Their thoughtful catering spoke volumes and made me feel highly valued. And therein lies the secret: any food laid on the table with love will work wonders.

THE MEANING AND SIGNIFICANCE OF COMMUNITY

It all started in the dining room known as the Wheelhouse of Stockholm Bird Observatory in 1977. This place would be dynamite in the hands of Christians, we said to each other. Peter was heading for ordination into the Church of England at the time, yet with a rapidly growing commitment to environmental issues, particularly the conservation and protection of birds. We were becoming increasingly alarmed too by the decline of the planet and the Church's apparent non-involvement in the crisis. Surely Christians, with their belief that the Earth is the Lord's and that responsibility for its care has from the beginning been entrusted to humankind, should be at the forefront of the environmental debate?

Gradually a vision was forming in our minds which encompassed both our concerns for the natural world and our longing to see lives changed by the love and forgiveness of Christ: a Bird Observatory; a residential centre for small groups of birdwatchers and naturalists, where, on the bridge of a genuine common interest, they could meet, live and talk with committed Christians and perhaps encounter something of the nature of God in a relaxed and unthreatening context.

We hadn't initially thought about working through community. But when we began to develop this into a project in which many different people were living and working in the same place, we stumbled on the richness of this way of carrying out our studies and our work and realised how important it is. And it seemed to us that the reason why working through community is important for Christians is that Christianity is about relationships, not about religion.

Some national organisations have drawn from the experience of Cruzinha, establishing a centre where team leaders, scientific staff, volunteers, visitors and local people live and work more or less together, along with assorted animals, the occasional injured bird and, for the really lucky ones, the odd snake cooling off in the fridge. But in some countries it is either impossible or inappropriate. In Lebanon, for example, multiple households, in two locations separated by forty miles of mountain road, have lived out a different understanding of community by sharing resources, meeting frequently in both places and working together over many years to manage and protect the same site in the Bekaa Valley. One might say that the worldwide family of A Rocha, along with the international team, trustees and friends of A Rocha, forms a dispersed community of sorts. Increasingly, a kind of virtual community is undeniably constituting itself, albeit invisibly. Our emphasis on community includes the importance of integration with a geographical context and building good relationships with other conservation initiatives and with the national and international organisations with which we collaborate.

I think the extended family model of community is still the most effective way of experiencing not only what a Christian conservation organisation does, but also why and how it does it. Everyone who works in conservation is committed to the study, understanding, protection and transformation of the natural world. In A Rocha centres, by throwing our lot in with a bunch of people who share our passions and goals and yet are very often different from ourselves, we discover that we ourselves are being transformed in the process, sometimes quite painfully, thereby offering hope not only for the planet but also for its people who are often blamed for causing the problems in the first place. Choosing to embark on a shared enterprise and to embrace an interdependent lifestyle with no convenient escape routes when the heat is on is somewhat countercultural and involves significant commitment and trust.

Genuine communities always need to extend themselves. As Christians we have strong reasons to believe and practise this, knowing as we do that all people everywhere share a common identity by virtue of being created by God, and therefore, in some way, bearing his image. We belong to the community of the created before joining the community of the redeemed. Committing to a group of people, making ourselves mutually accountable, trying to live as transparently as possible, inviting commentary on our choices and decisions, adopting others' ways of doing things because they're better than our own, recognising others' gifts and our own limitations – these things are counterintuitive and make us feel very vulnerable. Meals together, including preparation and clean-up, downtime, playing, laughing and learning to forgive create a wonderfully welcoming environment in which all kinds of people might truly feel at home. Community doesn't come about by having deep conversations over coffee; rather, those kinds of conversations are part of what is possible when people are already opening up their day-to-day lives to each other: peeling carrots, planting seedlings, singing to kids or fixing the bicycle chain . . . again.

Expressing the meaning of what we do through our relationship with God, with each other and with the wider creation speaks louder than any words, however eloquent. So by welcoming people into A Rocha communities, cheerfully accepting that they are more like building sites than five-star hotels, we are drawing them in to discover for themselves God's amazing love for all creation – including them!

All the visitors come with varying degrees of personal need. Many go away at the very least refreshed and strengthened, delighted by the birds, flowers and considerable natural beauty of the place – fortified too by Violinda the cook's superb feasts. Some go away having had a new experience of the God they thought didn't exist.

People understand what Christianity means when they can see how Christians live together. It's one way among many others that faith can take physical shape, physical form, become accessible to other people. Of course, before people become Christians or Buddhists, atheists or anything else, they belong to the fundamental community of the human family. And therefore, everyone ever born, I believe, is part of one common psychological community.

Unfortunately, many people's first encounter with Christians is an unhappy one, because they're often made to feel different, there's often an 'us and them' culture and people are made to feel as if they need to change in order to become part of the community; they need to become something different from what they are.

It is extremely important that those we're working with in the environmental world feel fully accepted and welcomed and valued as they are and respected as fellow human beings. There's a very strong theological reason for this.

It also seems particularly important for young people, who are often searching for reality in relationships, looking for intimacy, for a place to belong. It's particularly important for them to find places where they can take part in the research and in the field studies, and live among Christians, while being completely accepted for who they are. And in this way, they can learn about it from the inside. Sometimes we describe the life in our field centres as living 'inside out'. What's really on the inside of people and motivating their life and behaviour at work is something that becomes visible in the rush and pressure of work and relationship. And it's particularly compelling and draws people in.

I think people feel lonely and not only world weary, but word weary. Many of us have words coming at us from all directions all the time. We're being constantly bombarded by words. As D. L. Moody is believed to have once said, out of a hundred people, one might read the Bible, but ninety-nine read the Christians. We aren't making a coherent statement about what we believe unless we are close to one another, living and working through the difficulties when they arise rather than walking around or walking away from them. This is a very powerful part of A Rocha's work. As people who are involved with us begin to feel included and witness the depth of relationship between people, they start to experience God's love.

PHILIP'S STORY[6]

Thomas and I were sent into the city to make the preparations for the meal. I was glad to go. There was a strange mood among us, a pent-up anxious energy, and if we hadn't been given something to do I'm not sure I wouldn't have started a fight over nothing, simply for the distraction. Although it was only just after sunrise, the day seemed to have been long already.

The streets of Jerusalem were heaving. Jesus had told us to follow a man with a water jar, and by then we were happy to trust it would all work out. At first we just wandered aimlessly, but after a while we realised we'd have to concentrate. Nearly everyone was carrying something. Thomas said he thought he'd seen the man we were looking for and grabbed at my arm as he set off in pursuit. There was no trace of him, and I was playing out the scene in my mind where we had to go back to the others and ask for another clue, when we saw him entering a doorway down a side street.

When we called to him, he turned as though expecting us, a big welcoming smile on his face. Yes, he did indeed have a guest room and we were welcome to use it for the night. He led us up some stone steps inside the courtyard, and it was perfect. It was even furnished with low tables and there were plenty of cushions.

Judas had given us an unusually generous amount to spend on food. Jesus had been talking about this meal for weeks, rehearsing the dishes on long, hungry walks as we made our way from town to town until we were all groaning and salivating, and we knew he'd want the best and a lot of it. It wasn't our first Passover together, but there was something different about this one.

By the time we were done at the market we were laden like donkeys, lugging sacks of dried beans and flour, great bunches of rosemary, thyme and hyssop, bags of pistachios and almonds, olives, oil and salt, and, of course, the main event: the lamb. We had to go back for the wine. Thankfully the merchants had laid in good supplies – we weren't the only ones planning a big night.

The fire was stoked and hot by the time we were back with everything – the women of the house had been busy with their own preparations. We gave thanks for their presence many times through the day as they reminded us to get the beans on for the cholent early, to turn the lamb before it became charcoal, to stop eating the date charoset before it was all gone. Last to prepare was the bread, crisp and flat as the night our ancestors fled Egypt. And just as we stretched the last morsels of dough, there was noise and dust and the merry jostle of greetings and loud cries of appreciation at the smells and sight of the fruit of our day's labour.

We had lit the oil lamps and the upper room looked festive and inviting. Many hands helped to carry the loaded platters up the steps, laying them on the tables down the centre of the room. Once bags had been set down and feet and hands were washed, wine was poured into the stone cups our hosts had generously provided and we settled to eating, drinking and talking.

I was a little way down and across from Jesus, who had John on one side as usual and Judas on the other. There was an intensity to him that night. His eyes were brighter, his laugh louder. But I noticed there were moments he seemed to disappear within himself, distant and inaccessible. Sweat made the hair along his forehead damp, though the evening was pleasantly warm, not hot.

Suddenly he was on his feet, pulling off his cloak. I wondered if he had a fever. But then he called through the doorway for a bowl of water and a towel, and knelt behind Peter when a serving girl brought them to him. He tucked the towel around his waist and, to our horror, took Andrew's gnarly, dirt-engrained foot in his hand to wash it. We were stunned into silence, watching him as he worked his way from one to another, washing and drying with the tenderness of a mother and the humility of a slave. We were all waiting to see how Simon Peter would take it. He had that red, explosive expression on his face that meant he was going to make his opinions known.

'No, Lord. I won't let you. What is this?'

'You'll understand later, I promise. If you belong to me, I have to do this for you.'

'In that case wash my arms and legs and my hair too!'

We all laughed, the tension broken, and Jesus said something about most of us being clean enough, though not all of us. When he'd got around all twelve, he sat back down and explained that the foot-washing was meant to show us the way we were to look after each other. Then his mood darkened. One of us there in the room, he said, was going to betray him. We began glancing at each other, wondering who it was. We were a tight group. We had been through everything together, loved each other like family. I'm sure I'm not the only one who felt physically sick. I saw Simon Peter poke John in the ribs and John lean back into Jesus to whisper in his ear.

Jesus ripped off a chunk of bread and dipped it into the bean stew before handing it to Judas. 'Do what you need to do,' he said. 'Go. Do it quickly.'

Everyone up my end was trying to figure out what he meant, and most of us at the time thought he was off to get more wine. I think we were trying to protect ourselves from the truth.

By now it was fully dark outside and the oil lamps created little pools of yellow light. We were still eating because the food was in front of us, but no one was hungry any more. Jesus said a lot that night. Between us we remembered everything. He talked about leaving us, though not for ever. He said he was going somewhere and we would know how to find him there, that he'd leave us a Spirit who would help us. He reminded us of something we had all come to believe, that he and the Father are one and to know him is to know God. He urged us to be obedient to all he had taught us, to stay connected in love to him and to each other.

There was still a pile of flatbread on the table, and picking up the top one, he ripped it in two, saying as he did so, 'Thank you, my Father, for this bread.' After a pause, he addressed us: 'This is my body, broken for you. Whenever you eat this bread, remember me and what I did for you.' We silently took the pieces he handed to us, the taste forever linked in our minds to that moment.

The wine in his cup had long since been drained. He reached over for the nearest wineskin and refilled it, giving thanks and saying, 'This is my blood. It represents a new covenant, and I pour it out for the forgiveness of many. It will be the last wine I drink before I'm in my Father's kingdom.' As he handed it round, each of us taking a sip before handing it on, we couldn't bear to look at him. There was a dawning realisation among us that he wasn't speaking in parables or stories.

It was our practice to sing together once we'd eaten. He started us off, a psalm we sang often. And then, having brushed off the crumbs and piled up the dishes, we set out towards the olive grove and whatever the night would bring.

A PRAYER THANKING GOD FOR A MEAL

Lord God, thank you for the food before us. We know it is a gift, that you have once more provided what we need to live. We don't take it for granted. We are grateful.

Thank you for the soil, the rain, the seeds and the seasons; for farmers and fishers, flavours and textures, the mysterious alchemy that turns our raw ingredients into edible wonders.

Thank you for the people around this table. We are glad to be together. Bless our conversation as we eat, and draw us closer to each other.

Amen.

Miranda's journals

1996–1999

23 September 1996

I'm writing this in Beirut, Lebanon; poor, ravaged once-beautiful Lebanon. Landing in the middle of the night we were grateful for friendly and familiar faces and their introductions and explanations as we wove our way through the devastated and chaotic landscape of hurried reconstruction.

In six days we've covered most of the country, except the far north – even Tyre and Sidon in the south, just ten miles or so from the Israeli border. The roads are a nightmare; there is a heavy military presence in many areas, frequent army check-points and the not-very-distant sound of shelling a constant reminder of ongoing conflict. The situation here is very volatile, but there are plenty of exciting things going on too. We got the feeling the Lord is at work and A Rocha has a part to play in what he is doing. I feel ashamed to have prayed and understood so little about this part of the world.

18 October 1996

The time in Austria was wonderful. For the first few days I desperately wanted it to work out, finding myself strongly drawn to various people in the community, to the international student volunteers, to the exciting possibilities opening up in Eastern Europe and the beautiful setting. Perhaps more than anything else it was simply the idea of something that is already up and running — and they even had a house in mind for us, rather a lovely one.

However, we had prayed for clarity by the end of the week and, albeit by different routes, Pete and I were united in the strong conviction that we are not being called here – though there are all sorts of possibilities for fruitful collaboration. So France it is, although we are not much further on in terms of the specifics of how it will work out.

Recently, I think the Lord has been speaking to me about developing a habit of thankfulness and gratitude. I'm afraid I may have slipped into dissatisfaction, and grumbling even, or at least failed to embrace his marvellous multicoloured will for us with joy. I'm really sorry for that and am looking for grace and more grace.

21 November 1996

The whole of the first week in France has felt like a kind of homecoming. The time has been full of signs of the Lord's presence. Even the language is returning, albeit rather rusty and Portuguese-ified.

We've been very aware of the A Rocha family in Portugal, in Kenya, in Lebanon and in the UK at the sharp end of this work, as in different ways they take on new territory for the kingdom of God. And we've needed to pray such a lot as we've pored over maps, made phone calls and begun to contact people. In such a short time it's impossible to form detailed or accurate impressions of the various areas we are looking at, so we are relying very much on the Lord to meet us both in ordinary and extraordinary ways, and are praying constantly that he leads us to the right place and even to a house that we could rent when we return in mid February. This is an increasingly urgent need for the whole family.

We've been offered a two-bedroom home in Oxford and a car for use over the Christmas period. It will be our last family time for several months and we are praying very much that it will be special and will find the right balance in hospitality and 'just us' moments. I suspect the Lord is protecting us from ourselves by giving us only two bedrooms!

7 December 1996

We have a home! Yesterday we signed papers to rent a house on the edge of a village north of the Camargue and south of Avignon. We felt this area was by far the most promising environmentally, with an exciting combination of habitats and a host of possibilities for fieldwork. For two nights we stayed with some delightful nuns, being very blessed by the love, simplicity, stillness and prayerfulness of their hospitality. The village has a strong feeling of community and everyone we spoke with was unusually friendly, open and welcoming.

3 March 1997

Here we are, '*chez nous*' at last. The house looks quite tiny from the outside but, like the stable in the Narnia Chronicles,[1] it is much bigger inside. Lots of room for visitors! It has been such fun to put it all together. As we left most of our furniture and household stuff behind in Portugal, we have had to spend a bit of time getting kitted out again. *Most* of our belongings from storage arrived on the first Saturday. They seem to have lost four or five boxes, a couple of bookshelves and a little table. It wouldn't matter so much if they didn't contain many of our favourite things – special lamps, books, pottery, rugs and pictures. Even so, it all looks lovely and we can't wait to begin filling it up with people. In fact, I suppose that's already begun. We had a fine evening with three local couples on Saturday:

good eating, talking and praying and a fitting beginning to the hospitality of the house.

11 April 1997

As the dust settles and we dig in, the euphoria of having somewhere to live and being surrounded by familiar things again has given way to the hard work of enabling this new project to take root, and, as with Portugal, the ground is hard.

Finding French team members is a higher priority at this point than the actual building for a centre, but few old farmhouses escape scrutiny as we cycle past.

20 May 1997

Gauntlet has found and delivered our missing boxes. And Pete has made bookshelves to replace the lost ones with Beth as a carpenter's mate; the net result is a whole new feeling of settledness. It's really lovely and homely and the timing is perfect as the pace hots up and people begin to arrive to stay.

While we are so grateful for amazing financial and practical provision, not least for the sofa which means we now have somewhere to sit, how on earth do we reconcile our own essentially trivial needs with those of Zaire, for example? We can't square the circle but keep trying.

12 December 1997

It is exactly a year since our visit to France, during which, after eighteen months on the move, we found a good place to work, a house to live in and a second-hand car to buy, along with new brothers and sisters in Christ ready to welcome us with open arms as we planned our move. Today we received confirmation that we have our first French team member arriving in a few months. A historic moment and we are very excited about working together.

9 January 1998

I'm still getting the hang of sorting the feasting side of things in a new place and culture. The best our local supermarket could provide by way of a turkey was a 4½lb bird, more like a large chicken and a bit of a comedown after the 26lb monster Jem staggered home with from Oxford market last year. So I ordered a ham too, and was a bit taken aback when Pete went to collect it on Christmas Eve and returned with a vast side of pork instead. It lasted a whole week in various disguises.

2 April 1998

In many ways, this has been one of the most difficult months we can remember – a time for hanging on, really. Yet as the dust settles, I realise it's also been an amazing time for answered prayers, lovely phone calls, letters and a real sense of being prayed for by dear friends. I'm so thankful for the love of those around us and for the Lord's, which is patient and forgiving and never runs dry.

We had a wonderful time with Pete's mum and dad, even with the bleak cancer prognosis hanging over us. The lump in Dad's neck grew visibly while they were here and was quite uncomfortable, but he was happy throwing himself into all the practical jobs we never seem to get round to, so a lot of things work better than they did. We did lots of exploring together and had lovely companionable evenings. I loved cooking special meals for them. What next? We're not sure, but he sees the specialist again in a week.

A recent and painful problem in A Rocha has moved a long way towards being resolved, both personally and structurally. We are clarifying issues and protecting relationships, but it wouldn't be true to say it hasn't been very difficult at times. Good communication has been re-established and there is a sense of moving forward shoulder to shoulder (Zephaniah 3:9). For years, A Rocha was associated only with Cruzinha. Now it encompasses six countries and is an altogether more unwieldy beast. We all need wisdom, discernment, humility, prayerfulness and vision to see the way forward.

16 July 1998

Just over three weeks ago, Pete's Dad slipped into heaven. The Lord's timing, even in the tiniest details, has been extraordinary – perfect in a way that has made us all feel intimately known, loved and cared for. Pete and I arrived back from Canada in time to spend three very precious days with Mum and Dad, helping Mum care for him, talking, reading, praying, remembering, laughing and saying all those things we wanted to say, before Dad died on Tuesday afternoon.

The funeral, a week later, was a fitting celebration of a remarkable life and a real affirmation of the power of the resurrection and reality of heaven. Someone commented that it was so like Dad to make people laugh even at his own funeral. Jem read from *Pilgrim's Progress*, and no one in the church doubted for one moment that the trumpets were indeed sounding for Dad as he reached the other side.

8 December 1998

We are just back from our first visit back to Cruzinha, which is in tip-top shape thanks in part to a volunteer handyman. It not only looks wonderful but, even more amazingly, everything works!

It was quite overwhelming (good overwhelming) to spend time with many old friends in the village. We had no choice but to eat an incredible amount, and can now hardly walk! How humbling to discover that friendships not only survive but actually grow across time and distance. What a privilege to share meals, conversation and laughter with people whose experience of life has been so different from ours.

30 January 1999

Isn't life funny? Less than two months ago we had a call from the estate agent telling us we had to move, and now here we are, wood burner crackling, music playing, mistral howling – settled in number four as if we've been here all our lives! Pete is across the road with our neighbour watching the final of the European Championships, which I suspect may become a regular event. They are coming for aperitifs before lunch tomorrow.

30 March 1999

A Rocha seems to be growing and developing at breakneck speed internationally. Sometimes all the different sagas unfolding simultaneously feel rather overwhelming and we have been praying for peace amid tackling the mountain of ordinary and extraordinary things that arrive into each day. It is so important to find time for nurturing family relationships, welcoming visitors, getting to know local people, giving hospitality, nourishing our own inner lives and even house cleaning. All these things are imbued with meaning and filled with worship when their context is growing relationship with the living God and when they flow from his love and our increasing love for him.

18 August 1999

I have a strong sense of grace in my life. This is often painful, since it comes in the context of my limitations, frailties and sometimes downright selfishness, pride and folly. But it's also good news, of course, insofar as it is a sign of the involvement and activity of a heavenly Father who hasn't given up on us and who disciplines us as dearly loved children in a way that 'produces a harvest of righteousness and peace for those who have been trained by it'. I find myself remarkably often in Hebrews 12.

Jo has had a challenging month with a L'Arche community in Northern France, one of three young and untrained helpers caring for six quite profoundly handicapped adults. It has been good for her French, and she has learned a lot in other ways and done a lot of thinking and praying.

August is visitor month. We are into our fourth houseful – *full* being the operative word. It's very Cruzinha-like eating out under the vine together, especially when Portuguese is the dominant language. More of a crush when we get driven inside by ferocious mozzies!

15 November 1999

Today there was news of another major earthquake in Turkey, continuing wretchedness and misery in Chechnya and even serious loss of life and homes not far from us here in Southwest France because of the torrential rain and catastrophic flooding. It puts the events of our own lives in a different perspective. As does the unfolding story of a couple of friends' battles with cancer. I have been thinking about what it means to offer a sacrifice of praise. The bottom line is the faithfulness and sovereignty of God who is absolutely in control of all the circumstances, even if he doesn't always seem to be, and has given a solemn promise never to leave or forsake those who put their trust in him. The renewal of the earth and heaven is what we look forward to.

21 December 1999

A new millennium is about to begin. Some people say it's just another year, but it feels quite momentous to me. I love new beginnings. They are one of the things I love most about being a Christian, although thankfully you don't have to wait for a new millennium to be given one! This year has seen the family all over the globe, it seems. Pete and I have travelled more widely than ever for A Rocha, to the bemusement of our friends in the village. 'Off again! But why?' Well, we ask ourselves the same question sometimes and indeed hope to travel less once an expanded international team is established to help facilitate A Rocha's explosive growth. We hope soon to add to our French team to share the load here, especially in our absence. Five A Rochas are up and running with another four simmering away. That's why, if you look closely, the little shed in our garden that serves as Pete's office sometimes appears to be shaking with all the action! Estie has been in Brazil and Ecuador, Jem in Canada and Jo is thinking about what next after graduating from Birmingham next summer.

FIVE

THE CLEAN-UP

*Wash the dish not because it is dirty nor
because you have been told to do it, but because
you love the person who will use it next.*

ST TERESA OF CALCUTTA

I grew up in a home with human not mechanical dishwashers. While us children did some standard protesting and shirking, by and large we saw the benefits. There were usually many people around the table for dinner and the Cruzinha cook, Violinda, was a three-course kind of cook, so there was a lot to be cleaned. There were also, however, many hands to make the work light. These kitchen sessions were some of the best social times of my childhood, involving as they did all kinds of silliness, story-telling, advice-seeking and giving, and as I got older, shameless flirting with various handsome conservation scientists in the guise of dishcloth fights. If you take a tea towel, dip a corner in water and then twist it tightly and flick it you can really hurt someone while subtly conveying that you think they are quite attractive.

As I had such positive associations with the tackling of post-meal carnage, you might think I would have gone out into the adult world inclined to be the first to get up to my elbows in sinks anywhere and everywhere. But if you were reading this in earshot of any of the many people I lived with between the ages of eighteen and twenty-fine you'd hear a splutter of outrage. The truth is I was good at making mess and even better at leaving it for someone else to sort out. During my first year at university, I often left congealed pans sitting on the side for weeks at a time. Finally, and understandably, my flatmates reached the end of their communal tether. I got back from a lecture to find they had dumped the latest unwashed items on my bed in a rancid puddle of grey water.

After university, I moved to Canada for postgraduate studies, living in a large house packed with people. My Canadian housemates were by and large far too gracious and servant-hearted to confront me with my bad behaviour with either passive or active aggression. I would swan airily through the kitchen noting that yet again one of them had worked their way through a dish-mountain of my making. If the job was in progress, I was always sure to express my profuse gratitude. Tolerant and good natured though they were, I suspect there were multiple times they were tempted to dump great sinkfuls of greasy grey dishwater over my head. I would have deserved it.

Perhaps they will be glad to hear that poetic justice has been served up to me in heaping portions. My dear husband, I soon discovered, was more averse to washing up than I was. A stand-off ensued, during which our basement flat became hazardously dirty. Plates were wiped off as needed, to be immediately returned to the unsavoury pile of food encrusted items on every kitchen surface, including the floor. Our young marriage threatened to founder on the rocks of this seemingly irresolvable conflict, and so we reached an agreement. I would be the family dishwasher when it was just us. When we had company over, Shawn would take a turn. And he forked out for our first dishwasher (a model so primitive it had to be attached to the tap with a rubber hose every time it was used) with his personal spending money. This has been the situation until I had a major tantrum a few months ago and demanded a renegotiation of terms. We now have a family rota and a fully plumbed-in dishwasher.

I absolutely love cooking for people, but to this day I struggle with the mess it creates. Mess, sadly, is an unavoidable part of hospitality. It has become for me an opportunity for character growth and a deepening of my capacity for love and service. The outworking of faith is as much about how we do what we do as what we do. Paul's words about finances apply here too: 'Each of you should give what you have decided in your heart to give, not reluctantly or under compulsion, for God loves a cheerful giver' (2 Cor. 9:7). My ongoing task is to see the scrubbing of the pans, the rinsing of the glasses, the loading and unloading of the (beloved) dishwasher as an outworking of the Holy Spirit's enabling presence in my life.

As always, there are caveats and hedgings around any dishwashing principles we may be tempted to nail into place, such as the host must always take on the clean-up. On some occasions, the best kind of hospitality is the kind that says, 'You are part of the family. Please pitch in.' The most loving thing to do might be to socialise a person so they won't go on to annoy people by not pulling their weight. In a longer-term situation, if there isn't a sharing of domestic chores, corrosive resentment is likely to build up. So we must feel our way forward, looking for the best way to care for each person on each occasion.

There is, of course, more than just dishes cluttering up our kitchen after a meal. Food waste and packaging must also be faced. According to the Environmental Protection Agency, food packaging production has gone up by 200 per cent in the USA since 1960, amounting now to just under 100,000 tons, much of which ends up in landfill. Each year, around one-third of the food produced worldwide is thrown away.[1] If you were to have the pleasure of staying with my friend Caro, you would be served meals made with ingredients the age and condition of which are rarely seen outside a museum. She is in a very small minority of people willing to do what it takes to eliminate waste from the kitchen.

During the first couple of weeks of the COVID pandemic, there was mass panic about food shortages in the UK, which led to stockpiling and consequently an actual shortage of food in the shops. Shortly after, photos began to circulate online of mountains of mouldy bread, black bananas, packets of grey meat and bottles of lumpy milk on pavements outside houses up and down the country. Huge quantities of food were wasted because, out of fear, many bought more than they could store safely, let alone eat. Even under normal circumstances we are tempted to over purchase by 'buy one get one free' offers and a reducing 'per unit' price the larger the quantity. Nothing has been saved if we actually only need one bag of potatoes and leave the other to grow roots at the bottom of the cupboard.

Dave Bookless, Director of Theology and Churches for A Rocha International, first understood these issues to be of concern to God when, at the end of a visit to a beautiful island, he discovered there was no traditional waste collection or sorting on offer. Instead, he was instructed to take the week's accumulated rubbish and dump it over the cliffs into the sea. As he did so, he felt God whisper, 'How do you think I feel about what you are doing to my world?'[2]

Collectively we have done irreversible and horrifying damage to a creation God made from scratch and declared 'very good' (Gen. 1:31). We have polluted the air, poisoned the water, depleted the soil and decimated our fellow non-human Earth residents. Since the 1950s, as some of us have seen standards of living rise exponentially, we've turned a blind eye to the catastrophic consequences. We have brought the Holocene to an end – almost twelve thousand years of climate stability enabling the development of civilisation as we know it. Now in the Anthropocene, extreme weather events, mass species extinction, decreasing areas of fertile land are the new normal. Those who bear the brunt first and worst are those who are poor and powerless. How do we think God feels about that?

This is all extremely depressing, and I don't advise you think about it late at night or if you are at all emotionally vulnerable. Eco-anxiety is real and hard to dig out of because there is nothing very reassuring to hold on to. The more you know, the worse it gets.

You may assume that working for a conservation charity would be terrible for my mental health and sleep, but one of our distinctives in A Rocha is our stubborn insistence on remaining hopeful, and I am actually doing fine and generally sleep quite well, unless we are in the middle of one of the increasingly common heatwaves. Our hope is not in humanity's ability to address the crisis, or in what we believe to be an unbiblical idea that heaven is situated in a far-off non-material parallel universe, where matter doesn't matter. Rather, our hope is in God, our maker, sustainer and redeemer who has promised he will never give up on this beloved creation of his, however badly we mess it up. As my friend and colleague Ben Lowe so eloquently put it, 'This wide and wonderful world that we are a part of . . . is the very work of God's hands and so we trust that its future also rests in God.'[3]

And so, back to the mess in the kitchen. Will it save the world if we compost the vegetable peelings, recycle the tins, avoid where possible one-use plastic packaging? Clearly not on its own. But is it the right thing to do anyway? Yes. This is God's place and our common home, and he minds very much how we behave in it.

INNER MESS

Another kind of mess exists not just in the kitchen but in all the rooms of any house we go into, and outside too, because it is inside us. After all, as one wag put it, 'Wherever you go, there you are.' However glossy and well put together you appear, the chances are there are corners of your mind and heart that could do with some attention. The insecurities, resentments, judgements and dishonesties we all hide within us inevitably cause trouble in relationships, which is why working on our own stuff is the best thing we can do for others. It took me a long time to be convinced that getting therapy wasn't self-indulgent, but rather my best route to becoming a person able to love others healthily and well. Our mess is not a personal, private matter.

During my first higgledy-piggledy experience of community in Portugal, I quickly discovered that by far the most agonising emotional challenge was produced not by the blatant faults and failures of others but by my own acutely uncomfortable reactions to them. Sometimes the dis-ease persisted for days, long after the awkward customer had reverted to being a much-loved member of the family. You think you are a nice person, quite in control of your life, and suddenly a snarling tiger wakes up inside you when someone else has been difficult. What rises up inside you is far uglier than what provoked the conflict, and in a panic you realise there is no moral high ground on which to pitch your tent after all. Generally speaking, the most intractable and grating characteristics we encounter in others are the very enemies we wage war on in ourselves. We look not so much with scornful pity into the flaws of another but rather with dismay or even fear into the failures of our own.

'Man is not an arithmetical expression,' wrote Dostoevsky.[4] 'He is a mysterious and puzzling being. His nature is extreme and contradictory all through.' C. S. Lewis, peering inside himself and finding there 'a zoo of lusts, a bedlam of ambitions, a nursery of fears and a harem of fondled hatreds,'[5] appears to have reached an even more disturbing conclusion about the human condition.

The Bible says, 'If it is possible, *as far as it depends on you*, live at peace with everyone' (Rom. 12:18, italics added). We can't change the other person – they are always going to be irritating and hard to get on with – but we are responsible for being changed ourselves. As G. K. Chesterton is said to have written, 'What's wrong with the world? Dear Sir, I am. Yours sincerely.'[6] All of us are works of art in progress, pots on the wheel, and, as with any artistic enterprise, one often seems to go backwards, not forwards, creating more mess instead of the longed-for order.

There is an unhelpful theory that circulates around long-term singles in Christian circles, often perpetuated by insensitive older relatives: you are not married because you are not yet a perfect spouse for someone. Work on yourself, and when the buzzer goes off they will be there to pull you out of the oven, all done. A version of the same misguided idea persists around hospitality, and it must be rooted out and discarded (note: responsibly, in the correct recycling bin). Jesus never had a problem with people's issues. Look who he sought out and lavished his love upon: the demon-possessed, the walking wounded, the outcast, troubled and disturbed. And what did he have to say to the religious elite who appeared so very righteous and together? 'You hypocrites! You are like whitewashed tombs, which look beautiful on the outside but on the inside are full of the bones of the dead and everything unclean' (Matt. 23:27).

I have a rather disturbingly readable face; my state of mind is writ large enough across my visage for even a passing stranger to interpret. 'Cheer up, love! Might never happen,' they might feel prompted to call out. Or, 'Won the lottery? Cat got the cream?' My mental health comes and goes, I'm horribly sensitive, regularly over-estimate my own capacity and get over-tired, speak before I think, fall into deep pits of self-doubt, neglect my prayer life and try to soothe emotional pain with food and junk TV. It would be far easier to keep all these unfortunate aspects of myself hidden from view, but to do so would mean becoming a hermit. While a rare few may have that particular calling on their lives, for most of us, spiritual and emotional growth happens in the close company of others. We discover and develop our humanity as we bear each other's burdens and allow them to bear ours.

If you are holding back from setting a large table and flinging open your front door because you are afraid of exposing your less-than-perfect inner state, you are not the only one. Since Adam and Eve tried to cover themselves with fig leaves, the human instinct is to hide away in shame. Push through the fear, step into the light and you will find the God who sees all is not shocked or dismayed by the state of you, and he is at your right elbow, your co-host.

The key to loving others and living peacefully together is surely to begin to take hold of how much we ourselves are already loved. Henri Nouwen, who struggled all his life to experience this love for himself, nevertheless understood it well. He wrote, 'Long before your parents admired you or your friends acknowledged your gifts or your teachers, colleagues and employees encouraged you, you were already chosen. The eyes of love had seen you as precious, as of infinite beauty, as of eternal value.'[7]

This is a voice that has fallen silent or perhaps never spoken to many people's lives. When we understand that we are loved and have unique significance and value, we become free to bow out of the ruthlessly competitive and comparative culture to which we belong and offer the same forgiveness and acceptance to others that we have received. Before we are called to any action, we are called to accept that we are his.

RELATIONAL MESS

Mutual dependency and belonging is very difficult in a culture that places great emphasis on self-sufficiency and independence, actively discouraging the model of personal and economic interdependence we find in the Bible. We are used to privatising our experience of life and then placing ownership upon it: my family, my job, my money, my faith. Nowhere is this tendency more dangerous than in the community of believers, where isolating people from one another effectively denies the gospel its power to transform relationships and become visible in a world badly in need of some good news.

The concept of community is not so much absent as in need of redefining. Generally, it is assumed that community means people of like mind or compatible values choosing to live together. But we were to discover during the early years of A

Rocha's life in Portugal that genuine community can be created with people of similar, different or indeed no particular beliefs. It begins with inclusion; it involves love, acceptance and forgiveness, and it depends on a commitment to transparent relationships and self-giving hospitality, to a shared life of which the centrepiece is more often the kitchen table than the meeting room. Unconditional welcome is God's undeserved gift to us. We are not at liberty to introduce a different set of rules for those who arrive on our doorstep.

A former Archbishop of Canterbury, Dr Rowan Williams, addressing the General Synod of the Church of England, said, 'God calls, God makes a difference of such a kind that a community appears, bound to and in his Son by the Spirit's power.'[8] The apostle Peter's first letter to the scattered Christians instructs them to give hospitality to one another and to use the gifts they have been given for the common good, but above all to love each other deeply, or, as the Revised Standard Version has it, 'hold unfailing your love for one another' (1 Pet. 4:8). We need to reflect prayerfully on these passages that speak to us of the reality of God's presence in his people.

Conflict is inevitable in close relationships. Though few enjoy it, done well it leads to commitment, intimacy, joy and love. So how can we allow conflict to become a building block and not a roadblock of community?

The soil in which love germinates depends not on perfect performance but on forgiveness, not on avoiding mistakes but on readily meeting them and being quick to apologise. Of course, the need to practise forgiveness presupposes offence, often ugly and horrible and painful to bear – especially in ourselves.

Christians have an unfortunate tendency to prioritise being nice over being honest in the mistaken belief that niceness equates to godliness. But the most destructive form of conflict is the kind we pretend we are not having, the kind that goes underground and leaches into the water table.

My friend Helena was having coffee with a group of friends recently, when she noticed one of the women was refusing to meet her eye. Being a direct kind of a person, she pulled her aside and asked if something was wrong. No, no. Nothing at all. Except it clearly was. As parents of children in the same school and members of the same church, there was ample opportunity to confirm there was indeed a sense of excruciating tension in the air. Eventually, Helena had had enough and dragged this person out on a walk. A full year earlier, it transpired, Helena had shared a story about this lady's son in a group setting, unaware of the historic sensitivities around the incident in question. Rather than confront Helena with her sense of betrayal, she quietly decided to end their budding friendship and walk away. If we don't acknowledge wrongdoing, whether on our own behalf or another's, we short circuit the God-given mechanism for maintaining connection between fallen humans: repentance and forgiveness.

Good conflict presupposes a commitment to the relationship. It is worth having the occasional rough moment to strengthen bonds and clear the air, because for the sake of an easier hour or two we risk losing something of lifelong value. My sister Beth and I once had a terrible fight in which we both said some brutally wounding things just as she was about to leave and catch her train back home after the weekend. I will always be grateful she chose to miss it and stay to give us time to work things through.

As someone almost pathologically averse to interpersonal tension and yet wildly keen on cultivating friendships, I have had to learn a lot of hard lessons about good and bad ways of fighting. While I can't claim to have mastered these principles, they are some of the best I've come across: keep the focus of any conflict laser sharp on the matter in hand and don't drag in everything else you've always been bothered by. Use words that describe your own feelings rather than words that interpret the other person's motives or behaviour (for example, sad, angry or afraid versus manipulated, belittled or undermined).[9] Speak directly to the person in question and don't make others fight proxy battles for you. Address the issue as soon as you possibly can and don't give it a chance to fester. Breathe slowly and deeply and try not to shout. Shouting rarely helps. Pick your moment carefully – that Bible verse about not letting the sun go down on your anger doesn't mean in summertime you need to keep fighting until late at night when everyone is exhausted and can't think straight. Do your very best to understand the other person's perspective and try to give them the benefit of the doubt. They could be a vile and dangerous monster, but they are probably just a struggling human like you.

Lastly, we look for ways to learn from conflict. The people we most need to be among aren't always the ones who make us feel the most comfortable. However, it is always, and only, the truth that sets us free and enables us to change. So, it is not only the friends who are firm and encouraging who come to us as gifts of God, but also those who are willing to speak truth into our lives and then to be there as we embark on the untidy process of transformation.

Let's allow God to make us into a visible sign of his kingdom, a message of hope amid despair, a glimmer of light in so much darkness. Of course, the community we are really waiting for and for which we have been created is the new Jerusalem, coming down from heaven,[10] but that future begins here and now, and has power to refresh and inspire us to press on overcoming the temptation to withdraw, choosing instead to open our lives to each other.

JAMES' STORY[11]

We were all in a rather strange frame of mind during those days after the crucifixion, when we'd got the Master back and then lost him again. That might explain why we spent that night out on the boat. We weren't sure who we were or what we were supposed to be doing so we fell back into old habits, though it seemed like we'd forgotten how to catch fish. Hours we were out there, and nothing.

Peter was in a bad way still, beating himself up about bottling instead of going to the cross with Jesus. When we first saw Jesus after the resurrection, Peter was as overcome and happy as everyone else. But I noticed he hung back. There was such a crush, it wasn't like they could have a heart to heart and sort it all out then, but I could tell Peter needed to know he was forgiven by Jesus – directly and with no room for doubt.

When the night's darkness became the grey of early morning, we began to row wearily back to shore. It was completely still and the only thing breaking the water was our oars. That's why we could hear the man shouting to us when we were still at least a hundred yards off. 'Morning, friends! No fish?' Perhaps he'd seen our dejected postures. 'Put the net out the other side – see what happens.'

Thomas and Nathanael hauled the net up into the boat, dripping cold water all over me, which I wasn't best pleased about. But then a second after they'd heaved it off and back into the lake, everything was chaos. They were nearly pulled in with the weight of a churn of frantic fish trying to escape the net. We were caught between belly laughing and trying to get a grip of the ropes to land the catch, and then John was shouting, 'It's him! It's the Master!' and Simon was off, neck deep and ploughing through the water like a man possessed, trying to reach him. He'd grabbed his cloak first, and I remember noticing how odd it looked puffed up with air around him before it became soaked and clingy.

The rest of us carried on trying to pull in the net for a minute or two, before we figured we'd better just tow it behind us. I'll never know how it didn't break. Peter and I counted up how many fish there were, just to stop us fighting about it later – I knew he'd exaggerate, and he knew I knew. Anyway, there were 153.

We were all keen to get to Jesus so we just fixed the net, fish and all, to the back of the boat and pulled it onto dry ground. Jesus had a fire going and fish already on the go, and he was almost hopping with the fun of having surprised us. We were a bit quiet, though. Speaking for myself, I felt a bit foolish for not having recognised his voice. And there was still the oddness of having watched him take what we all obviously thought was going to be his last breath just a short while earlier. I'm trying to say it felt a bit funny. There wasn't the easiness we'd had around him before.

We sat around the fire getting warmed up and waiting for the fish to cook. The lack of food and sleep made me a bit blurry and I kept wondering if Jesus would still be there after each blink of my heavy eyes. The way he'd been coming and going recently meant it was entirely possible he'd be gone in a puff. I couldn't bear it, so I kept staring and staring at him through the pale dawn light as the fish skins blackened and the smell grew painfully enticing.

The sun finally appeared over the hilltop and made the lake's surface glint and sparkle. You could hear our stomachs growling by the time Jesus handed round the food. I've not had a better meal before or since. It was our normal gritty bread, a slab each serving as plate for the hot, smoky fish, but the fear that had made it hard to swallow since the arrest in Gethsemane had gone. We'd added a few big tilapia we'd caught to the ones Jesus was cooking. It was a proper feast.

Nathanael and I admitted to each other afterwards that we wanted to ask him, 'Who are you?' but didn't dare. We knew it was him; it was just he'd come back different, and we wanted to check and be sure. We'd seen him three times by then, it's true, but I don't know – he'd come out of that tomb changed.

Peter was the first to finish, and he jumped up muttering something about going to check on the boat. We were all glad when the Master followed him. We understood why he was beating himself up, but we could tell he'd been forgiven and we hated seeing him all twisted up and miserable, not least because it made him a bit of a beast.

A moment after the two of them set off along the beach, John was after them. He had this thing about not missing out and he liked to think he was the favourite. 'The One Jesus Loved' he called himself – I kid you not! Now and then it bothered us but mostly we just gave him a hard time about it. We knew Jesus loved all of us. At least John had the decency to stay a couple of paces behind this time, though, so Peter could get things sorted out.

Apparently, Jesus really pushed the question of whether Peter loved him. He asked three times. That must have hurt. Peter was the first of us to really see who Jesus was, and other than that one night his loyalty hadn't wavered. But I think Jesus just wanted him to understand how strong that love was going to need to be. It wasn't said in so many words, but John said Jesus had basically hinted about the way he would die, and it wasn't going to be of old age in his bed.

At that point, Peter took a step back and nearly fell over John. It was pretty entertaining from where we were sitting. Peter says he asked Jesus what was going to happen to John. Other than the fact that Jesus told him straight it was none of his business, the two of them don't completely agree on what else was said. Peter seems to think he implied John was going to live on until the second coming, and because he's such a loud-mouth that's the story that's got passed around. But John's smart, and he said Jesus' exact words were, 'If I want him to remain alive until I return, what's that to you?' He's right – nothing there to say he's not going to die. I guess we'll see what happens, anyway.

A PRAYER ABOUT CONFLICT

Lord God, you want us to live at peace with each
other, to be unified and loving so we can represent
you to the world. You know how bad we are at that!

Please forgive us for finding fault, withholding
grace, withdrawing affection when
differences and problems arise.

We need your Holy Spirit to help us find
a way through. We need to be better at
saying sorry and letting go of grudges.

Thank you for the gift of your patient love, showing
us there is always hope because you are with us.

Amen.

Miranda's journals

2000–2008

20 January 2000

Eight young friends descended on number four for New Year's Eve, ranging from Estie's East German friend who she met in Ecuador to our artist friend with her 6'4" boyfriend, and various of the kids' school and university friends. I cooked a nine-course meal for New Year's Eve. It was a first for me – it's the timing that's the challenge. Everyone put on their poshest gowns and blackest ties. We had readings and table games and praying. Then up to Daudet's Mill to let off our truly pathetic fireworks while admiring everyone else's impressive ones for miles around. We lay on our backs in a circle, marvelling at the brightness of the stars, and then danced in the village streets. Pete and I were tired earlier than the others and, coming down next day, I found they had all stayed up until 3.00 a.m. clearing everything up. What stars! On New Year's Day we cooked sausages and played football on the beach. It was a very special houseful of people.

1 May 2000

I have felt in the eye of an emotional and spiritual storm these past few weeks – partly because of a number of friends in situations of acute suffering, but also having the family so dispersed, and the change of gear in our working life to more travelling and speaking, meeting lots of new people all the time. The absence of a close Christian friend (other than Pete) to talk and pray with probably increases a sense of spiritual isolation and loss of bearings. I have an amazing array of soul mates but they all live rather far away.

We are told that in all things — including the valley of the shadow of death, betrayal, rejection, emotional turmoil, *whatever* — God is working for good.[1] I can hardly begin to understand this, but I know it is true.

22 June 2000

'And you also are among those Gentiles who are called to belong to Jesus Christ' (Rom. 1:6). This verse came up in lights for me this morning as I made a list of all the things that need doing. Before any calling to *do*, we are called to be God's dearly loved children, belonging to Jesus, made to love and worship him and to do what he has prepared for us to do (Eph. 2:10) with trust, confidence and perseverance.

6 September 2000

The A Rocha leaders' conference was such a rich week – eleven nationalities, many different languages as we worshipped and prayed together, so much joy and gratitude to see young people who joined A Rocha as students now manifesting wisdom, grace and maturity, leading national projects. What a faithful and creative God we have. Many commented on the united, committed and loving ambience.

27 September 2000

A man Pete met and talked to on a plane a few months ago (mainly about his soul, not fundraising, he says!), has offered to buy a centre for A Rocha France. He apparently owns a couple of French villages. We know this man very little and have only his word to go on, so we are praying it comes to pass.

A friend of Pete's from school and his wife came for supper this week: baked peppers, the surprise addition of whiting as an experiment, salmon with baked Provencal vegetables, potatoes gratin, green beans, cheeses, pavlova and lots of good talk.

15 January 2001

We had a wonderful few weeks with all the family home and many friends staying over the Christmas and New Year weeks. The weather was more soggy than usual, so there were fewer walks and more games and talking and some good films. We even read aloud *Twelfth Night*. And now everyone is dispersed to the four corners again and we are adjusting to our other life, wanting very much to learn to trust God more to learn about grace and to be more love-filled people.

15 March 2001

A Rocha continues to grow at a pace that would be alarming if it weren't so evidently the Lord who was doing it: Bulgaria, South Africa and Finland are in the process of establishing projects, with Brazil and India not far behind. Christians around the world are waking up to the fact that 'the earth is the LORD's, and everything in it' (Psalm 24:1) and we will give account to him for its wanton destruction.

However, 'mission' for us this week has involved days of trawling the many second-hand furniture shops to equip the lovely French centre we've been given. As a team, we resolve that this whole process should be part of our worship and witness and not merely an inconvenient distraction from the real work, so we have prayed a lot and been amazed and delighted by some of the specific and detailed ways the Lord has met our needs, not least in providing a lovely Moroccan Muslim woman who, as I write, is sitting in the common room sewing loose covers for old sofas and armchairs and making curtains.

12 May 2001

The week in Lebanon was so good in every way. We have an exceptionally gifted and committed team working in the Bekaa Valley, often under enormous pressure and in extremely isolated circumstances. It was incredibly encouraging to see progress on all sites since our last visit and to see the village flat up and running so well as a centre of sorts. We participated in some ringing, observed a school visit to the Marsh and attended meetings in Beirut.

We are having an open evening at the French centre next week and have invited everyone we know, including many of the people we've met through finding furniture, the builders, plumbers, et cetera. It will be great to have a chance to explain who we are and what we do.

In all the comings and goings of visitors, the shopping, cooking, changing beds, cleaning bathrooms and being present to those who come (one or two recently with very big burdens and needing more time and attention than usual), I'm aware I need to make more time to pray and read and think and be still.

16 October 2001

Needless to say, the appalling events of 11 September put all our small struggles in a different and probably truer perspective. The goalposts really have moved and the world feels a more precarious place. We were unable to fly to DC on 13 September as planned, but managed to get on the flight five days later. Some events were postponed and, of course, it was a poor moment for creative fundraising initiatives or even following up some of the exciting contacts. Everyone is too distracted and upset and many are personally connected with people who died. We are praying for justice and peace and for the wisdom and integrity of world leaders.

17 January 2002

'In the morning, LORD, you hear my voice;
in the morning I lay my requests before you
and wait expectantly.
(Psalm 5:3)

As I read this verse just now, I realised that I'm better at part one (laying my requests before him) than part two (waiting in expectation). So one of my resolutions as the dust settles over the old year and rises in clouds over the new is to do more waiting and more noticing, as God generously and faithfully continues to answer prayers – even the ones that never find words but form nonetheless in heart and mind.

13 September 2004

This last trip was full of contrasts – one minute sleeping on a friend's dining room floor with foreign students coming and going all night, the next in a tiny room in the Pickwick Arms just a few minutes' walk from Fifth Avenue New York, listening to the incessant wailing of sirens and clamour of voices in the streets, then the five-star sumptuousness of The Ritz-Carlton for the fundraising gathering. Finally, we slept in our friend's childhood bedroom in Lima, wallpapered from floor to ceiling with many years worth of front pages of 'Fauna de Péru' — all those avian eyes watching us fall asleep! Despite the distracting and unfamiliar sound of the city at night, we slept better than we had at 8,150 feet above sea level in Vail, Colorado.

Our friend's mother, Eva, made us a breakfast that first morning of smooth, sweet porridge, papaya juice and coffee ground in the garden, and afterwards, Juan, his father, accompanied us on a tour of the small, private park shared by the neighbourhood houses. He is ninety-three, very deaf, multilingual, mentally sharp and the only surviving brother of twenty-one siblings.

He has planted many trees in the park over the years; his palm tree planted about forty years ago from seed must be almost twenty feet tall. We were dismayed to discover that he poisons the cat population to protect the birds – it's interesting where different people draw the lines. He digs substantial holes in the grassed area too, to stop the kids playing football.

The conference was from 4.30 p.m. to 9.00 p.m. each day. It was moving to see the A Rocha Peru team in action. There was a lot of hanging about at the gates of the museum afterwards, waiting . . . for what? Just waiting. And talking . . . and eventually heading off to find something to eat.

One night we were booked to speak to a group of young Christian professionals about A Rocha and to have supper together. We arrived at least an hour late but, as Peter commented, again and again throughout the week we were grateful for our years in Portugal and what they taught us about the importance of people and protocol and the unimportance of plans.

25 October 2004

We have had almost two whole, blissful weeks at home in Fontvieille. A couple of huge thunderstorms greeted our return, clearing the muggy atmosphere. Today there is a lovely smell of woodsmoke in the still, autumnal air, and robins, blackcaps and black redstarts are filling the garden with song and hopping through the brilliant red vine.

We've been catching up with ourselves, our sleep, our neighbours and goings-on with the French team. There are fourteen Dutch volunteers over there, replastering and painting the common room.

Pete continues to carry the very heavy burden of finding the funds for this incredibly fast-growing A Rocha family, but he, too, has loved being home and managed to rest – at least at weekends. So often we feel like David standing before Goliath. For him, a heart for God, a passion for his glory and one smooth stone in the right place was enough.

10 December 2004

How thankful we are to eat and drink a host of weird and wonderful things, and to receive truly heart-warming hospitality in a multitude of varied settings. Asia is amazing! And hot, very hot, with something like 85 per cent humidity, but everywhere indoors has aircon there these days. Thirty-five years since Pete's last visit to Bangkok, it wasn't possible to revisit many of the old haunts, but we did meet up with one of his friends from the student centre where he spent his gap year, now a pastor and Bible teacher in the city, and had supper with him and his wife and family.

31 January 2005

Today, along with the rest of the international team, we are fasting and praying about the financial brick wall A Rocha is currently facing and asking the Lord what he is saying to us. 'We Africans are *used* to miracles!' said Bihini Won Wa Musiti, from the Democratic Republic of Congo, one of our trustees. Another trustee, Alfredo Abreu, writes that he is not too worried about our present troubles, as hitting the wall 'wouldn't make sense in the light of who God is and of his long-lasting guidance and provision for our A Rocha family'. And our chair, Matthias, reminded us that our problems are the problems of growth, success even, and we must learn to trust God more than ever as he leads us into new things.

Meanwhile, God is continuing to bring us amazingly committed and gifted people to work with! Part of our current task seems to be to help and not to hinder these people. Whatever the challenges and pressures – and for a few months now they have felt intense at times – it is always inspiring and encouraging to meet together as a team.

I expected to pray with intensity through the list of our particular concerns, but instead found myself drawn to several Bible passages. James 1:17 came first: 'Every good and perfect gift is from above, coming down from the Father of the heavenly lights, who does not change like shifting shadows.' I was struck by the constant, dependable, rocklike, sturdy and unchangeable nature of our God.

Then came Psalm 115. I spent much of the day mulling on sections of this. We need God to answer these prayers not for the sake of A Rocha's survival, or even success, but for his glory – because he is loving and faithful. Verse 3 put me in my place: 'Our God is in heaven, *he does whatever pleases him.*' From then on, the focus is on what pleases him, what he is like, how we can please him, and not on our needs, pressing as they are. In contrast to the idols, God has mouth, ears, nose, hands, feet and voice. He hears, speaks and acts, and when we see him we shall be like him. Repeatedly we are told to trust in the Lord who is our help and shield (i.e. provider of all necessary good gifts and protector from all harmful influences and obstacles). The utter folly of trusting anything or anyone else!

How, then, do we pray? Expectantly, I'm sure, not losing hope when the answer takes a while to come. And maybe even with the careless confidence of a small child who clambers onto her mum's knee, knowing that there will always be a hug, however busy she is. Psalm 115:12 says, 'The LORD remembers us and will bless us.' This seemed to come up in lights and, as if to underline the message, it is repeated three times: 'he will bless . . . he will bless . . . he *will* bless those who fear the LORD – small and great alike'. We are undoubtably among the small, and the promise extends to us too, so verses 14 and 15 are a great prayer for the growing A Rocha family:

> May the LORD cause you to flourish,
> both you and your children.
> May you be blessed by the LORD
> The Maker of heaven and earth.

God has not forgotten us. He will bless us. I do believe that soon he will open his hand and send his Spirit. I think a time of gathering is coming. There has been quite a lot of waiting!

The final passage I felt clearly drawn to was Deuteronomy 8 – warnings to the people of Israel about the dangers of times of abundance and success – e.g., phew, we can stop being so intense about our relationship with God now. All that praying and fasting was perhaps a bit over the top. And anyway, we did work incredibly hard networking and writing proposals, making phone calls and so on. When God answers all the prayers and the coffers are full again, we shall be just as dependent and needy as before. Praise the Lord.

17 June 2005

Three days ago, early in the morning, quietly and peacefully and characteristically without drawing attention to himself, my dear, dear dad slipped out of this world and out of all his suffering into the presence of God. Although he never lost his deep sense of unworthiness, he knew he would be welcomed by name.

He was an amazing man. Very early in my life, without realising it at the time, he incarnated the love of God, which I was later to discover, by holding me in his arms and stroking my hair with infinite tenderness and complete acceptance despite the fact that in my sleep I had been suddenly and violently sick. That image will never leave me.

15 January 2006

I've been feeling quite scattered and rootless; the constant comings and goings take their toll and sometimes I feel I'm just skating over the surface of the many worlds we inhabit. I need some time to review, reflect and recharge. We are trying to understand what God is calling us to at this point, what the shape of A Rocha should be and the shape of our own lives within it.

14 April 2006

Lately I have been reminded so often of the preciousness of friends. The decision to see more of them more often seems to be working well so far. Currently we have staying with us Sally from the UK, Jill from Portugal and Ginny from the US. Our neighbour Henri is quite envious of Peter with his four ladies!

Lots more visitors are lined up for May, June and July. We have to be quite disciplined to keep normal life ticking over. I reclaimed my shed in the garden and banished Pete to his office over at the centre.

We are just back from Kenya where we were able to fit in four days of safari joined by five wonderful A Rocha colleagues. One, Albert, is a manic and extremely knowledgeable birder. His passion for small-winged creatures hiding in dense vegetation ensured that we didn't get distracted by herds of large mammals lumbering by! The Big Five agenda was properly subverted, though I did get to see twenty lions so I can't complain. It was a wonderful and rich time in each other's company.

8 September 2007

Wales was uncharacteristically sunny for our family week in early August, and it was a wonderful time together with all the familiar ingredients – great walks and beach days, swimming and boules and barbecues and fun evenings all squished around the kitchen table.

Towards the end of the week Pete's back 'went' and he gave us a big fright by having an addisonian crisis and ending up in hospital for twenty-four hours. Having no adrenals, his body wasn't able to cope with the acute pain and he passed out. The ambulance arrived in time, and he recovered quickly. We have learnt a lot, not least that severe pain needs careful handling, and we must always travel with injectable hydrocortisone. We each have a kit, with one in the car and, thanks to Bethie, the qualified nurse in the family, we know how to use them!

It has been important to debrief the episode with some dear medical friends. It's generally agreed that the patient works out what happened and moves on, whereas the nearest and dearest who witnessed the event tend to need a bit of time to process.

21 May 2008

Pete has taken Jo and Alexa to the airport after their week with us, and Estie and baby Jack are staying on for a few more days. I've discovered I'm not as good as I thought I was at multitasking, but overflowing ironing baskets, toppling in-trays, crumb-strewn floors and strange-smelling fridges never killed anyone. It's been a brilliant if chaotic family week and we've loved getting to know the fifteen-month edition of Alexa, even while we pull random objects out of the loo and replace the contents of emptied cupboard drawers.

Working out the balance between family and work is challenging and sometimes stressful. It probably isn't wise to combine elderly and super wealthy donors with very small grandchildren and exhausted mums, which is what we did on Monday night this week. But in fact, as with so many of Pete's high-risk strategies, it was a howling success even if I was a nervous wreck on the day. Our visitors were enchanted with Jo and Estie and there was a lot of fascinating conversation, including easy and open sharing of our faith, and Jo was able to engage very deeply with one of them whose daughter suffers with serious depression.

Among the guests was an extremely wealthy American who lives nearby for part of the year and has taken a shine to us and to the work of A Rocha, about which she is becoming passionate. She is a high-profile philanthropist with the means to help us in a very big way. It has been a privilege to get to know her and her friends, most of whom are barons or ambassadors and probably never experienced simple Christian hospitality. It's amazing how much spiritual hunger and openness we've encountered already.

The trustees have asked us to focus more on building relationships with current and potential donors through hospitality, as well as travelling to promote the cause generally and being advocates for the work of A Rocha specifically. More support could transform the work of A Rocha worldwide, not least funding leadership positions in many of the projects. And, of course, it is also a mission field in its own right.

We are loving the new emphasis of our work and having more people coming to stay, for meals and for visits to the A Rocha France centre and study site, but I also feel on quite a steep learning curve. Fairly predictably, I'm tightening my seatbelt and taking pills for vertigo, while Pete is standing on one of the wings shouting, 'Faster! Faster!' We both realise we need to be deeply rooted in Christ for all this and to spend serious time in Bible study, thinking and praying. I had a wonderful retreat in April and thought a lot about rooted-ness and fruitfulness. I felt the Lord was saying to me, 'I am all you need.'

SIX

THE FOREVER FEAST

*Now at last they were beginning Chapter
One of the Great Story which no one on earth
has read: which goes on for ever: in which
every chapter is better than the one before.*

C. S. LEWIS, *THE LAST BATTLE*

We have dreamed up the occasion, issued invitations and prepared ourselves, our homes and a whole lot of food. We have grown hungry, and our guests have too. We have welcomed them at the door and ushered them inside. When the meal was ready to serve, we have seated everyone around our table, where each one had a place. As the wine and the food has done its work, the conversation has risen and fallen in its natural rhythm, punctuated now by a burst of raucous laughter, now a gentle silence. The Spirit of God hovered over the waters, a creation moment; a place of belonging was woven from strands of kindness, time and hearty victuals.

The kingdom of God is both now and not yet, and so all good things still come to an end. We find ourselves standing here in an empty kitchen, the dishwasher humming quietly, the most daunting pans soaking in the sink to be faced tomorrow, or maybe the day after. Snatches of conversation replay in our minds, vignettes of atmosphere – too ephemeral to catch on camera, still lingering in the air with the smells of cooking and lemony detergent.

This is an emotionally complex moment. There is nothing quite as satisfying as hosting an event that becomes more than you could have hoped for. An evening around a table with people who – with the help of candlelight, delicious food and unrushed time – catch glimpses in each other of the beauty God sees in them is nothing less than a foretaste of heaven. And now there is an emptiness in the house. There is a nagging sadness that trails you as you get ready for bed. There is a loneliness born of separation from this family that formed for an evening, or a week, or a season, only to be summarily disbanded and dispersed.

Hospitality can be as swift and simple as a shared flask of coffee on a train or as life-changing as welcoming a refugee family to share your home for a year. It can be the decision to put your phone in your bag on your lunch break and give your full attention to a work colleague in distress, or whipping up a gourmet four-course dinner to celebrate a friend's birthday. Whatever shape it takes and however long it lasts, it invariably concludes with goodbyes and separation.

I absolutely hate goodbyes. They were the hardest part of my childhood, full as it was of hellos. The Cruzinha community was in constant flux, some joining for years, some just days. Even short-term household members could make a big impression. I remember forming a deep bond with an eighteen-year-old visitor called Joy when I was eight. We went blackberry picking together and she helped me make some clothes for my doll. Although she only stayed for a long weekend, I still remember crying into my pillow so hard when she left it was still damp at bedtime, hours later. With boarding school when I was thirteen came goodbyes of an order of magnitude more painful, as four times a year I left my family, my home, my country and my climate for sometimes months at a time. Every airport arrival was overshadowed by the knowledge I'd soon be there again to get back on the plane to take me away.

Then came the final goodbye to Cruzinha and Portugal, as our family moved on to new adventures – for me, a year in Zimbabwe, three years at Birmingham university and four years in Canada. Shawn and I met in Canada and got married in the UK, as the most convenient location for the largest number of people. I had not considered the fact that when we drove away from our wedding reception I would be waving goodbye to a crowd of beloved friends and family for an indeterminate period. At that stage the plan was to make Canada our permanent home. Poor Shawn had to deal with his brand-new wife weeping her way through their honeymoon and early weeks of marriage. Our decision to move to England was made on the basis that living there would make a good proportion of goodbyes far less dramatic as we'd be close enough to have regular meet-ups with at least half our family – Shawn's being mostly in the States. We do have to learn to live with separations minor and cataclysmic and everything in between for now, though. Even marriage vows include a cruel reminder of the long goodbye awaiting us, joined as we are only 'til death do us part'.

Back to where we were, standing in the empty kitchen. In some senses this is an ending: hospitality is, by nature, time-bound, and each episode, however protracted, comes to its inevitable conclusion. The relationships cultivated do not end, though; they continue in the gaps. There is a sense in which we create room for each other inside ourselves, tucking people into our minds and hearts and carrying them with us as we go about our separate lives.

Sometimes a person takes up a massive amount of space, squeezing out our ability to focus on or care about many others. This form of hospitality can be costly, too, and an equally precious gift to its recipient. I know that for the days and weeks following Mum's death I had friends who held me in their minds and prayers around the clock. Because they did, I didn't feel alone in my grief for a second, not least because of the many messages I received reassuring me I wasn't forgotten. Sending even a brief text or postcard maintains connection despite physical distance and continues to maintain and even build relationship. The best and deepest of these, we have biblical reason to believe, stretch out before us into eternity. That tug of longing for someone, whether they live around the corner or have departed this life, one day will be soothed by a reunion that isn't overshadowed by a future parting.

When hard things happen, sometimes the only driftwood to keep us from drowning is God's firm promise that the worst the world can throw at us is not worth comparing to the life that is to come. It is important that our hope in heaven is firm, because often we don't get our happy ending here and now. The treatment doesn't work, the depression never lifts, the longed-for child is not conceived, the wrongly convicted dies in jail, the refugee lives out their days in the camp. 'If only for this life we have hope in Christ, we are of all people most to be pitied,' said Paul (1 Cor. 15:19), and he was right. Unlike humanists, for whom the best chance of happiness is in the here and now, Christians can absorb the worst the world can throw at us in the sure knowledge that one day it will be a speck in the rear-view mirror: 'For our light and momentary troubles are achieving for us an eternal glory that far outweighs them all' (2 Cor. 4:17).

What do we know, then, about this eternal place of glory? As a small child, I had some ideas about heaven, one of the most outlandish being that we'd all speak French: 'Bonjour! Bienvenue au paradis!' God would say, and I would magically understand what it meant. I'd also picked up the impression that it would be a state of cool airiness, bright yellow light, and the echoey sound of ghostly choirs endlessly riffing off the word 'Holy'. I was not at all impatient to get there, especially as my earthly life was pretty nice most of the time.

If you have ever had similar fears that you are heading to an endless existence in an echo chamber with no walls, the good news is that this is not at all the way the Bible speaks of what life after death will be like. And while we may have been given scant detail to go on, we have enough to trust it will be emphatically embodied and fully physical. The picture painted in Scripture portrays a restored and redeemed and not pulverised creation, where God dwells among his people in unveiled glory.

The idea that 'spiritual' implies immaterial comes from Plato, not Paul, who assures his readers they will be reclothed in flesh made for permanence – 100 per cent decay resistant: eternal life-long guarantee, living forever in his beautiful world (1 Cor. 15:42). And why would we not consider the entire universe to be part of God's long-term plans? As Virginia Stem Owens puts it:

> Where else can one draw the line between sacred and profane except around all the cosmos? For 'profane' meant originally outside the temple, and all creation was in the beginning, a temple for God . . . Still, we take the big black crayon in our hands and draw these little islands where we will let God live in the world . . . little concentration camps for Christ.[1]

All of this leads me to believe in heaven there will be proper face-to-face time with Jesus, reunions with long lost loved ones unspoilt by impending departures, meandering hikes in the deep silence of ancient forests, splashing and playing in crystal-clear blue lakes, summitting snowy mountain peaks bathed in a spectrum of colour our pre-resurrection eyes couldn't see, bear hugs and heart-to-hearts, gardening, birdwatching and painting, exploring and resting – all the good things made even better. And, of course, eating and drinking the finest fare in the best possible company.

FOOD, GLORIOUS (HEAVENLY) FOOD

You may have deduced by now that I am a great food lover. I wake up happy if I know there is crusty bread, butter and marmalade in the house. An invitation to dinner on a Friday will cast a glow as far back as the Monday morning before. I may not be able to resist humming with joy if the flavour in my mouth is particularly lively, say lime juice, chilli, fresh coriander, soya sauce and a hint of sesame oil. And yet, however full my stomach, however brilliant the cook, there's an emptiness that follows every meal as predictably as night follows day. Food and drink: they assuage hunger and thirst, bring delight and restore strength. The tastes, aromas, textures and colours testify to the goodness of creation. But we know they can't meet our deepest longings. A relentless craving persists.

God in his brilliance has given us the opportunity to experience on a daily basis how the very best of what this earth has to offer is but a foreshadowing of what he has prepared for us to experience in the renewed earth.

Jesus was constantly pointing towards a future existence in the presence of his Father, where we would experience the kind of satisfaction we can only dream of. 'Half of Earth's gorgeousness lies hidden in the glimpsed city it longs to become,' writes Robert Farrar Capon. 'For all its rooted loveliness, the world has no continuing city here; it is an *outlandish* place, a foreign home, a session in *via* to a better version of itself – and it is our glory to see it so and thirst until Jerusalem comes home at last.'[2]

The most common picture for heaven in both the Old and New Testaments is of a feast. While I am sure there is real food awaiting us, the heavenly banquet is a metaphor, not a sign that we can look forward to a never-ending eat-all-you-like buffet. Why this metaphor? What does it tell us?

Food, then as now, was a major preoccupation of the poor, its production and preparation more time- and labour-intensive than anything else. Even the rich were only as safe as the next good harvest. In this life, we can never guarantee the next meal or a constant, safe water source, and without them we soon die. But in heaven, death is no more, and food and drink are no longer a question of money, status or power, but of the generosity of God. This is the invitation:

Come, all you who are thirsty,
come to the waters;
and you who have no money,
come, buy and eat!
Come, buy wine and milk
without money and without cost.
(Isaiah 55:1)

The prophet Isaiah goes on to say:

On this mountain the LORD Almighty will prepare
a feast of rich food for all peoples,
a banquet of aged wine –
the best of meats and the finest of wines.
(Isaiah 25:6)

This is not a picnic of leftovers or cheap ready meals shoved in the microwave. God is pulling out the stops in the way you would only do for a highly honoured guest, no expense spared – the cellar scoured for the most valuable bottles, the prize animals butchered. When the long-awaited Messiah came, he set a table with a place for everyone – his life the price of entry. At this feast, supplies never run out. There is enough for all and enough for ever.

By the time of Jesus, there was a religious elite doing their utmost to erect and reinforce barriers to entering God's banqueting hall. The sacrificial system was so ramified and complex, only the most educated had a chance of understanding it, let alone being cleansed of sin. Every finer point of Law was policed, from festival observance to rituals of hygiene to tithing. One Sabbath, when Jesus was eating at the home of a prominent Pharisee and observing the fellow guests, he threw out a challenge: 'When you give a banquet, invite the poor, the crippled, the lame, the blind, and you will be blessed. Although they cannot repay you, you will be repaid at the resurrection of the righteous' (Luke 14:13–14). His persistence in dismantling the social and religious structures was one of the things that inflamed the religious leaders the most, stirring in them a murderous hatred which spoke volumes about their hearts. 'Whoever comes to me will never go hungry, and whoever believes in me will never be thirsty,' Jesus said (John 6:35).

In the book of Revelation, the Bible's great crescendo, we find our trinitarian God as host, guest and food all at once. He is there ready to come in and eat with us (Rev. 3:20). He presides over the celebratory feast for the marriage of his Son and the Church, his bride. He has offered himself up to feed us. 'At the marriage supper, love is celebrated in all its joy, and faithfulness is celebrated in all its firmness,' wrote Eugene Peterson. 'The marriage supper of the Lamb is all this, with the additional factor that it is God himself who is the meal.'[3]

I was blessed to be raised in a home where there was ample food on the table each night. The memories come thick and fast – Mum bright-eyed and triumphant, lifting a vast and perfectly bronzed turkey, stuffed front and back, from the oven for a

Christmas feast; in a checked apron whisking a white sauce with one hand while holding a glass of wine in the other, quizzing me about my latest teenage crush; squeezing in a couple more chairs and plates around the table under the vine for unexpected arrivals on a hot late summer evening in France; laying out an adventurous cheese board and sneaking slivers to try because cheese was the one thing she couldn't resist. She taught me to lead with the heart, to find space for one more person if at all possible, to put food in pretty pottery dishes even though it would mean more washing-up, to receive God's good gifts with joy, pleasure and the deep gratitude they deserve. In short, she taught me everything I know about hospitality, and much of what I love about Jesus. I miss her and I can't wait to see her again.

ENOUGH LOVE TO SATISFY

If you stand in the stillness of a country night, face upturned to a star-studded sky, allowing your eye to be drawn further and further into the velvety darkness, you will discover that what appears to be an inky black backdrop is merely a veil. It dissolves beneath your gaze, not so much drawn aside but thinning out, revealing tinier, more-distant stars which lead you, the earthbound astronaut, on a journey into space. Then you blink. And when you open your eyes and focus once again on the canopy above your head, the zillions of microscopic pinpoints of light have vanished, leaving only the biggest, brightest ones assembled on the stage.

A cosmos of unimaginable grandeur lies beyond the scope of human perception, the faintest hint of what can only be attained by the effort of concentration, and then only fleetingly. But thanks to unbelievable advances in technology, images from the Hubble permit us to glimpse a universe of some 50 billion galaxies blowing like snowflakes in a cosmic storm. In just a speck of sky, you can observe an astonishing collection in various stages of development, some dating back more than twelve million years. And the Bible tells us that God knows every star by name.

It was on such a starlit night in November 1972 that I stared into the darkness from the window of the top floor of a Victorian terraced house in Cambridge, searching out the distant stars as if they could shed their brilliant light on my dark musings. All around me the impossibility of verbal communication was being compensated for by what my grandparents might have called canoodling, some cheerful shouting and a good deal of heavy drinking. Thin plumes of blue smoke rose in the semi-darkness from incense sticks and cheap cigarettes. The music got louder, bodies closed in on each other and, alone on the bed by the window in a self-inflicted exile from the tactile crowd, I gazed into the night, magnetised by its sharp and clean purity, a single sentence forming in my mind, repeating itself again and again: 'There must be more than this; there *has* to be more than this.' Had my hearing been less impaired, perhaps I would have heard my own name included in the roll call of the stars.

I had arrived in Cambridge confused about faith. The year in France had shown me that I had inherited a strong set of principles from my God-fearing parents and, in particular, a very high view of marriage, but nothing that could help me overcome my insecurity or reassure me that I was deeply known and loved. As Augustine said, 'Thou hast made us for thyself and our heart is restless till it rests in thee.' While outwardly I was plunging into the heady freedom of student life in the early 1970s, inwardly I was restless and unresolved, questing, without knowing exactly what for.

My first day at college threw this ambivalence into sharp relief. 'Are you a Christian?' asked a striking third-year girl with shining eyes who seemed interested and concerned even by the state of my soul.

'Yes,' I replied unhesitatingly. Then, suddenly less confidently, 'Er, no.' Pause. 'Well, I don't really know.'

Through her and a group of equally radiant believers, I was introduced to someone alive but invisible, called Jesus. It was all rather baffling at first, but the cheerful acceptance and uncritical love shown to me by the student group was real enough. I certainly hadn't learnt to love myself that way.

It wasn't many weeks before the incoherence of my life led to a moment where choices became inevitable. The party proved to be the catalyst: that same night, weary of the tug of war inside and persuaded at last that I was all in or all out but not up for pitching my tent on the middle ground any longer, I prayed a very feeble prayer, to which God – whose hearing is certainly not impaired – mercifully responded by replacing the accumulated tension with a palpable peace and rocked me like a babe in arms while I drifted off to sleep on the hard floor of my room, my bed occupied as it was by others.

Once you know you are lovingly made, intimately known and absolutely forgiven, you can begin to take the risk of getting to know this person whose body you inhabit. Acquiring self-knowledge is apparently a painful and life-long process. I remember at the age of seventeen or so drawing immense comfort from the irrational belief that when I reached twenty-one the emotional turmoil would magically give way to a state of serenity and invulnerability to the vicissitudes of life. Whoever endowed that random chronological milestone with those mythical powers? Now I note that the illuminated panel above my head still recommends that I keep my seatbelt securely fastened as the turbulence is not over yet.

One of my favourite postcards depicts two cheerful women advancing arm in arm, and underneath the caption reads, 'A friend is someone who loves you even though they know you.' Of course, the Bible pulsates with the same message, culminating with the shout that rings across the universe: 'I love you anyway, you poor, sad, deluded creatures – I LOVE YOU!'

MARTHA'S STORY[4]

My brother Lazarus was at the meal – how that was possible is a whole other story. I will tell it to you if we have time, but you mustn't interrupt or there won't be. This meal, no, it wasn't at my home, but you can see where it happened from here. That big house at the end of the street. Do you see?

There were many people at the supper, held in Jesus' honour, and I was helping serve because the women of the house couldn't manage on their own. I was glad to help – every time I came in with another dish, refilled a cup, I heard a snatch of Jesus' conversation, caught his eye. When he'd last left Bethany we'd all wondered if we'd see him again. How could one man be so loved and so hated at the same time? Although he was among friends on this night, he had many enemies, and we knew they had tried to kill him – and would again.

Mary had been helping in the afternoon, but as dusk fell and the guests began to arrive, she disappeared. She's still good at that! The evening went on and the men at the table seemed to be enjoying themselves, laughing and talking as the spiced wine flowed and we brought in platter after platter of grilled fish, cucumber salads, olives, dried fruit and nuts, honey and yogurt.

I smelt what had happened before I saw or heard anything. The whole house was full of such an intense smell it made some of us sneeze. Like that, yes! Through the arch I could see Mary kneeling by Jesus, a white stone jar lying beside her. She had tipped the whole thing over his feet and everyone other than Jesus was standing, shouting, holding their noses, waving hands in front of their faces. Lazarus looked green in the face, like he might be sick. It was the same fragrance we had used when we prepared him for burial. Why did we prepare him for burial? Well, because he had died. That's why it was strange he was at the supper. I might as well tell you that bit now.

Mary noticed first that Lazarus wasn't looking right. He came in for the evening meal one night a bit pale and we sent him to lie down. By the next morning he was burning hot and complaining of a terrible pain in his head. We were worried enough to ask our neighbour to send his son to find Jesus and tell him, though we knew he was far away, on the other side of the Jordan. I'm ashamed to say it didn't cross my mind that we were asking him to put himself and his disciples in harm's way. We had no hope but that Jesus would come before it was too late.

But in the early hours of the second night, as Mary and I sat awake, one on each side of him, Lazarus gave a few noisy gasps and stopped breathing. Yes, we did cry. We were very, very sad. Lots of our friends and family came from Jerusalem and we were all sad together.

It was five whole days after that that Jesus reached us. Lazarus had been in the tomb four of them, but you will think I was out of my mind when I tell you I still thought there was hope. Jesus had given a little girl back her life, he had stopped a storm over Lake Galilee, he had healed lepers and cast out demons.

I heard he was coming and went out of the village to meet him. Mary wouldn't come. She was sitting on the floor all curled into herself and I couldn't move her. As soon as we were close enough to speak, Jesus said to me with an urgent force, 'Your brother will rise again.' I thought he meant on the last day. I wanted to find that comforting, but in truth it wasn't. Mary, Lazarus and I were everything to each other. I couldn't begin to face the idea of life without him. I had come to understand the importance of really listening when Jesus spoke, so even though I was in a state, shocked and overwhelmed and desperate to see him do something to fix this horrible thing that had happened, I paid attention as he kept talking: 'I am the resurrection and the life. Anyone who believes in me will live even if they die. Their life will never really be over. Do you believe me, Martha?' I told him I did. I believed he was the Messiah, the Son of God, the one we

Jews had been waiting for. Then we stood there a while, just looking at each other. I will never forget it.

He wanted to see Mary, and I went back to get her. Once she realised he was so close by, she came quickly, everyone else trailing behind her noisily. We do like to wail when someone dies, you're right.

You could see Jesus flinch at the sight of her, her eyes so red and swollen she could barely see where she was going. And then Jesus was weeping too, part of this sea of grief we'd been swimming in. You would never know he was about to bring Lazarus right back to us, as good as new.

We made our way to the tomb, and he told us to move the entrance stone. Everyone protested at once. You can't begin to imagine how terrible bodies smell after four days. You are right – we had covered him with perfume, but believe me, perfume doesn't help once a bit of time has passed. Jesus insisted, though, so in the end a couple of men heaved it out of the way.

'Come out, Lazarus!' Jesus shouted. We watched in stunned silence as this figure wrapped head to toe in strips of cloth stumbled towards us.

That was just a few weeks before this meal, so you can see why Lazarus might have had a bit of a reaction to the scent of the nard. But Lazarus wasn't the one who seemed most disturbed – it was Judas Iscariot. That one, you've remembered rightly. He was practically spitting with rage because, he said, Mary had wasted something that could have been sold and the huge amount of money raised given to the poor. On the surface it sounded a reasonable argument, but the other disciples told us later that they all knew he just liked a lot of money in the purse so he could help himself without much risk of being caught. I think Mary expected me to be angry with her, too, for the extravagance, but I would have done the same if I'd thought of it.

I never heard Jesus speak as sharply to anyone other than a Pharisee as then. 'Leave her alone,' he said. 'This perfume was to have been for my burial. You'll always have the poor, but you won't always have me.'

You never met Lazarus. He died – again – before you were born. And I was sad, yes. I miss him still, dreadfully. But as I told Jesus, I believed him then and I believe him now that the life he gives goes on beyond the grave. So, we will meet again. There will be more suppers with him and Jesus at the table, with you too, and me. The Messiah has opened the way and we will travel it to his side.

A PRAYER OF BLESSING

Written by Miranda in a card to her dear friend Annie

I'll be praying so much for you and feeling very
close to you and may the Lord cause our paths to
cross again 'ere long. Meanwhile, may he cause
his face to shine upon you, his peace to reign
in your heart, and his love to wrap you around
always, keeping you in his ways which are LIFE.

Amen.

Miranda's journals

2009–2019

15 December 2009

2009 has been characterised by waiting. It seems God has been teaching us to wait more patiently and trustingly, especially for his perfect timing. Clearly, we are not there yet. A couple of nights ago we were informed that the operation to repair Peter's torn knee cartilage had been scheduled for Monday in Oxford — yes that's this Monday, three days before moving to the amazing house we've been lent near Cirencester to host eighteen of our family over Christmas. I stomped around the village here in France, thinking about how to care for everyone away from home, including Pete's bereaved brother and boys, a sleepless family with a tiny baby, two toddlers, a pregnant daughter and various other exhausted young adults with an unfamiliar kitchen and a post-operative husband who won't take painkillers. What kind of perfect timing is that? Well, God was merciful to me and by the time I got home twenty minutes later it had been rescheduled for 6 January, altogether more doable.

The longest wait of the year was for the birth of sweet little Charis who arrived on 30 October. Alexa has become a very shiny big sister and remains a complete delight to the rest of us. Charis does great days and terrible nights but sometime soon she'll sleep through and Jo won't get a wink wondering if she's okay and waking every half an hour to check. It's that waiting again – for sleep this time – and trusting that the Lord will come and meet our needs.

26 May 2010

It's a perfect May morning here in France. Everything seems to be singing or humming or buzzing or blooming, and I have swapped the winter and summer clothes around at last. Only ten days ago we were still lighting the wood burner in the evening.

The USA trip last month went very well, and all its component parts. We pray that the investment in relationships at many levels bears fruit in terms of both more biblical thinking and consequent transformation, albeit slow, of people and places, and also in finding the financial and practical help A Rocha so badly needs. The quail and the manna keep coming and I think we are gradually learning to work with what we have rather than dreaming of what we could do with more.

Last week I was reminded that plans are only provisional on this unpredictable planet, when my flight home was cancelled owing to the Icelandic ash cloud. The extra six days in and around Washington DC became quite an adventure as I presented God with my blank sheet each morning and he proceeded to write poetry on it.

Times with people I hadn't expected to see felt like appointments – rich and deep encounters it would've been such a pity to miss. I came home spiritually refreshed and encouraged with raised faith levels.

Moving to England in a few months will bring big changes for us. Mum has suddenly become much more frail and is now only able to walk short distances and with a stick. Getting her sharp and brilliant mind onto the same page as her failing body is really challenging for her. I will need to budget plenty of time for her as well as for the kids and grandkids. More people will drop in, we'll be part of the church and easier to reach. There will still be some travel and hospitality to donors as well as colleagues, friends and family. Surprisingly, perhaps, we both feel entirely peaceful about the move, maybe because what seems to be needed is so way beyond anything we ourselves could organise! We've been reading *The Message* recently and came across this in chapter 3 of Galatians: 'The person who lives in right relationship with God does it by embracing what God arranges for him. Doing things for God is the opposite of entering into what God does for you.'

12 September 2010

Autumn migration has begun. Pied flycatchers have returned to the garden and, in a two-week period, spectacular numbers of south-bound swallows are roosting in the reedbeds of the Vallée des Baux. Meanwhile we are preparing for our own migration north, albeit not travelling so light. What a privilege it has been to call this lovely village home for the last fourteen years. Most of our mornings start with an early bike ride; at this time of year the ditches are full of purple loosestrife, the sky is black with gathering swallows and the air is sweet with the smell of over-ripe figs. Today we took a flask of coffee and marmalade sandwiches up to a high outcrop of rocks and spent some time thanking God for his amazing kindness to us over the last three decades. It feels very sad to be moving on, but also very right.

It is with great joy that I can record that an American foundation has made a major donation to our leadership fund that will build capacity for both the international team and nearly all of the twenty national movements around the world. We are full of thankfulness.

8 December 2010

We didn't have any angels or stars to tell us where to go or how to get there but, as if by heavenly satnav, God has led us to a lovely Edwardian semi, just a ten-minute bike ride from Mum's nursing home. It has everything we need, including a two-metre round table and a magical room for the grandkids with a wardrobe painted like a lighthouse.

7 July 2011

The last three months have been incredibly full. We've had lots of people come to stay and for meals, we visited family and friends and discovered that the house works brilliantly for the grandkids as we had hoped. Being around the corner from Mum is a perfect arrangement and we see her almost daily. Somewhere in the middle of that we have been to France twice, and Portugal and Canada once each. I have been practising deep breathing exercises. At breakfast today Pete told me he was afraid he was turning into one of those exotic creatures in Ezekiel with four heads, trolleying around in a manic fashion. Like the owner of the *News of the World* newspaper, I declined to comment.

14 December 2011

A few days ago, on the 10.17 a.m. train from Pewsey to Paddington, I settled into my reserved seat and began working on a report to the A Rocha management team about our recent trip to Malaysia.

'Are you Miranda Harris?' said a voice next to me. 'I recognise your handwriting!' It was an old friend and Cruzinha volunteer and I don't think we've seen each other for fifteen years or so.

That set me thinking about handwriting and about old friends. Reviewing this last year, it is the gatherings around our big table or the fireplace that have provided the best memories, and I am filled with thankfulness.

28 June 2015

We are just back from the A Rocha Leaders' Forum — this time a hundred of us from twenty countries gathering in Portugal for five days. When we are together, I often find myself asking, 'Is this a meeting or a reunion with friends?' For the first time we opened up a space for lament, acknowledging the groaning of creation and the pain of struggling against the relentless tide of destruction. But there was lots to celebrate, too, and the worship and Bible teaching have never been as powerful and uplifting, or relationships so deep and joyful.

25 October 2015

I sometimes feel quite overwhelmed by all the people I know and love and despair of honouring these precious friendships. The long and lengthening list of names on the fridge for whom I try to pray daily all have cancer. Even without extending more widely to the terrible suffering of migrants and refugees, this too feels overwhelming sometimes. My daily immersion in the Psalms is a wonderful reminder that stability and peace don't come from circumstances but from our maker, the sustainer of the universe, who, like the mountains encircling Jerusalem, surrounds his people and still has plans for us and for the world.

12 November 2015

This year has rushed past like the Chinese bullet train we took from Shanghai to Nanjing ten days ago, which travels at 310km/h. In the early 1970s we were involved in a student prayer group for China, so it was very moving to actually be there forty years on, not least a visit to Amity Press which has printed more than 140 million Bibles since 2008. We were invited to Shanghai to participate in a four-day seminar on the Bible and the environment. Listening to twenty-seven academic papers, mostly in Chinese with simultaneous translation, was challenging. One or two of the gastronomic experiences were too; I'm not a fan of jellyfish or cow's throat, but it was only a few days ago that we discovered we'd eaten earthworms as well! Raw blue crab, seaweed and fermented cabbage were on the menu in Korea, washed down by rice wine (think thick, slightly fizzy soup). We learnt to smile appreciatively as there was great generosity in the hospitality and wonderful fellowship. We visited our friends in Singapore, Malaysia and Hong Kong as well, to make the most of the long journey.

26 July 2016

Just over a week ago we celebrated our fortieth wedding anniversary with a few days on Mull. How have so many years passed that fast and with so much blessing?! The undeserved goodness of God poses a constant theological question, given so much suffering in the world. We pray almost daily that out of the incredible generosity of God, we will know how to be truly generous people.

The family staged a surprise party to celebrate – the grandchildren all burst out of the porch of Saint Mary's where we were married in July 1976 with shrieks and clouds of balloons as we made our entirely unsuspecting way up the path to the church. We sat on a bench in the churchyard looking over the sparkling bay to Tyrhibin where I grew up, eating cream teas and drinking Prosecco and feeling very thankful.

14 May 2017

We feel very much at home here in our village and increasingly embedded in our local church and community as so many relationships develop and deepen, especially with elderly, bereaved and seriously ill neighbours and friends. We are loving the growing area of work with A Rocha of spending time with potential young leaders. The travelling is very tiring and often challenging, though in terms of the work is still deeply satisfying. The next few months are particularly mobile: Hawaii for the World Conservation Congress, California, Hong Kong and Singapore, Australia and New Zealand.

9 January 2018

So good to be back in Fontvieille for this visit. It is 10:30 a.m. We have read Psalm 77 and prayed, walked around the village, popped in to Délices de Daudet for a hug with Cathy and a baguette, and into le Jardin de Florette for goat's cheese and figs, had breakfast and hung up washing. I'm eager to get to everything else. Pete does this so suddenly – abruptly even – that he plonks his laptop down in the middle of the debris I am in the process of clearing and vanishes completely inside his head! But such unhurried time preceded this change of gear. I am a blessed and happy woman.

4 March 2018

I have taken the big file 'Writing' off the White Room shelf and, to my surprise (and I confess cautious excitement), find substantial content for eleven chapters. I had got much further than I thought before sidetracking to help P with *Kingfisher's Fire* and Jo with hers. I feel the sap rising again, along with all the self-doubts and vulnerability that is never far away. Lord, I give this project to you. If the impulse comes from you, and the many people who urged me to write are truly reflecting that, I will need much self-discipline, perseverance and courage. Perhaps this is a *kairos* moment? Hesitantly I embrace it, but please lead and direct so that if it does see the light of day it won't just be my story but rather our story.

Sitting in the kitchen at BH, T & J have gone to work, Pete is out for an interview and I need to be working on talks for next week. Please steady my heart and mind and help me find the thread. Please help me to be attentive, and to focus. The two minutes silence is hardest, but here is what I became aware of:

the dishwasher quietly churning
cleansing and forgiveness
the warmth of the Aga behind me
God's comforting presence and love
the ticking of the clock on the wall
the gift of time *chronos* and *kairos*
the smell of the coffee – another great gift! –
but reminds me too of the fragrance of Jesus
the chiming of the grandfather clock
God sets us in families – I am so blessed in mine.

3 August 2018

I have just heard from Debs that our wonderful friend [universally known as] Poppa died early this morning. 'Lord, now lettest thy servant depart in peace.'

4 August 2018

It was a strange and sad day. I know beyond any shadow of a doubt that all is well with Poppa, all the anguish and wrestling and painful remembering is over, any regrets and anxieties finally washed away – the sadness is for the remainers. Life becomes a lot less complicated and anxious for the family, but our own small world, our own share in this remarkable clan, feels suddenly a bit grey and draughty. How we shall miss our Sundays, the Scrabble, the Six Nations, our endlessly interesting and stimulating conversations with every member of the family. I remember one lunchtime when he and Peter Moses, not yet two, were the only ones left at the table quietly talking to each other. We talked about sport and politics (trying to avoid anything beginning with T or B!), history, the war, church and spiritual matters, and, of course, the family – the subject closest to his heart which could barely contain the fierce love for each one, it seemed. He was so interested in everything and everyone, his intellectual and emotional reach was vast, and his memory, not least for the details of our own family and all things A Rocha, far surpassed our own right up to the end. He always prayed for our trips and wrote wonderful emails. I shall never forget the years of the pub lunches that he and I shared. We shared so deeply soul to soul and I know they were a comfort to him, but for my part I often wished I had a small recorder or even a notebook to ponder the many profound, wise and insightful things he said. We only saw the best of him, I know, and he of us, but oh how very good that best was. I always felt so proud in the company of such a courteous, gracious, handsome man.

15 September 2018

Dave slipped away early this morning. The Lord has prepared the way over the last few weeks and answered so many prayers. Lord Jesus, hold Anne through these early moments in her bewilderment, disorientation and exhaustion. Thank you for her incredible strength, endurance, courage, tenacity, faithfulness and love. Thank you for the deep friendship that has grown between her and me over the last couple of years. I rely on you completely to show me how to love and support her now, and I will pray and listen for your prompts, but without you, I don't know how to help. Give me inspired thoughts and words, gestures and actions, and thank you, Lord, so much for what feels almost like a training in loss and grief over the past few months. I'm so glad for Dave waking up in his brand new body, but I hope he gets to keep his beautiful smile!

John Wyatt's book *Dying Well* has just arrived. He says the hardest part is saying goodbye to those we love most dearly. 'Death would not be so bitter were it not that love makes life so sweet. Nor would death inspire such fear and dread were it not that it cuts us off from those whom we love, and who love us.'[1]

12 December 2018

Last Sunday I held a very small baby in church while her mother went to collect the other children. She lay still but alert in my arms, small dark eyes exploring the periphery of her still-blurred vision before settling on my face, the faint upward turn of her mouth bestowing a smile as stirring as the Advent hymn that enveloped us both.

We are all invited to move closer to another tiny child, more miraculous still – God himself contained in a newborn baby, eternity captured in time. The mystery and marvel seem to deepen each year. I have been thinking quite a bit about time recently. 2018 has gone so fast – I feel quite breathless to be on the threshold of Christmas again.

I love this season, though; the expectant waiting of Advent, the childlike anticipation of the birth of Jesus, the hope of light arriving in the middle of whatever darkness surrounds us and the delight of reconnecting with friends, so few of whom we manage to see in the fulness and fastness of life.

For many people, of course, it is a sad and lonely season, and for us too there has been sadness this year. Four precious friends died over a period of three months in the early autumn, including Poppa, who over the last seven or eight years became close family to us, joining us every Sunday we were home. I have understood a little better that grief includes losing someone who *loves us* as well as someone we love. The world loses a little of its warmth and comfort. I have been consoled by the God who created and controls time; he sent his Son in the fullness of time and he was the cosmic expert on the timing of all things, though so often it doesn't feel like it. 'My times are in your hands' (Psalm 31:15).

21 January 2019

2019 feels different. It is probably mostly because it's our last full year of paid work for A Rocha, so the next question comes in the background like a faint but constant noise which you hear whenever there is a lull in all the other noise. Looking back over the last four decades we see the faithful leading, provision and protection of God, often in amazing ways, and especially at the times when it felt like a bit of a wild ride. There have been lots of transitions, but this one feels longer and bigger than most, needing more than the usual wisdom for choices and decisions, and trust and courage for the unexpected. At times in recent months I have felt more fundamentally unsettled, though never in the sense of doubt in God's control over all things and his incredibly reliable goodness and love. It's more myself I struggle with. Sometimes it's hard feeling things so deeply, though this is something I am more often really grateful for.

I am working on living well and the rhythms of creation, cherishing family and friends, making good decisions about hospitality, measuring energy levels well and not worrying about medical things but being alert to anything needing action. Learning to grow old gracefully.

4 October 2019

It was so special to be back in Newport. More than anywhere else on Earth it encapsulates personal roots and history and touches somewhere so deep and fundamental that being there is more of a spiritual than a physical experience. It's as if I'm drinking in the glories of the landscape, the softness of the air, the smells of the sea, the subtlety of colours. And yet the more I drink the more thirsty I become. So much beauty, so many memories, and consequently so much praise and thanksgiving. It didn't rain until the very last day. In fact, the first two days were sparkling and warm, even on the beach at the foot of the sand dunes. Every day I went for long walks.

24th October 2019
This was Miranda's last journal entry. It was written in a notebook that was pulled from the water. Once dried, it was still legible. She'd been using an App called 'Pray as You Go' and some of what she wrote referenced Bible passages it covered that day.

Lord, so far on this trip I have felt held in your peace, enabled and equipped, confident and steady. This (as you know!) is not always the case; often you have rescued me, and surrounded me with songs of deliverance.

THANK YOU for your mercy, grace, strength, presence and peace, and for the amazing people who pray so faithfully for us. We are so blessed.

I lean into your love and faithful presence today, relying completely on you for wisdom and love. Fill us up again, inhabit us wholly, so we can please you, bring you glory and be a blessing.

Christ, light of the world; whoever follows him will have the light of life. Abraham was empowered through faith, and gave glory to God. His trust was reckoned to him as righteousness. All we have to do is believe in the resurrection.

2 Timothy 4:9–17. Luke was Paul's only travelling companion on a hazardous journey. Paul, with only Luke by his side, defends his faith. God rescued him from the lion's mouth.

'The Lord will rescue me from every evil attack and will bring me safely to his heavenly kingdom. To him be glory . . .'

'But the Lord stood at my side and gave me strength.'
Psalm 32:6–7:
Therefore let all the faithful pray to you
while you may be found;
surely the rising of the mighty waters
will not reach them.
You are my hiding-place;
you will protect me from trouble
and surround me with songs of deliverance.
I will instruct you and teach you in the way you should go;
I will counsel you with my loving eye on you . . .

Psalm 33:20–22:
We wait in hope . . .
he is our help and our shield.
In him our hearts rejoice,
for we trust in his holy name.
May your unfailing love be with us, LORD,
even as we put our hope in you.

INTENSIVE CARE, SPOKEN TO VOICE MEMO
7 November 2019

How can I bring you back
Brightly again
Into this room?
Dearest of all,
Miranda, most admired,
Most beloved.

Your charted voyage
Set off from the bridge,
With the Atlantic
Just to the south.
Coldest of seas,
But as you never tired
Of living and talking,
Most productive of oceans too.

We always loved Kit Smart,[1]
Poor, mad Kit Smart,
Who in his nature quested for beauty,
But God, God sent him to sea for pearls.
You have certainly gone for pearls now.

But I know that the birth of the new creation
Is truly found in deepest darkness
Where we are free at last
From the times that hold us.

I have to tread carefully here,
Because there is no marriage there,
As Jesus told us.
I will be treading carefully,
But will need more help.

Each dimming day will carry in its darkened womb
An absence for us all, not just me.
But just imagine beginning all of that
When we were twenty-two and three.

Peter Harris

AFTERWORD

Mum made marmalade every January without fail, enough to last the full twelve months. Marmalade-making seems like the kind of thing that should be passed down the generations, so this year my two sisters and I made our first attempt to keep the tradition alive. Delia said it wasn't wise to make more in one go than the quantities in her recipe, but what does she know? I bought enough supplies to make six times as much.

After several hours of squeezing and chopping, our fingers were shrivelled and stinging and the two giant pans dangerously full, even without the main ingredient (not oranges, but sugar, it turns out). Slopping sticky liquid on the floor, we managed to carry them to the stove, which wasn't strong enough to heat such vast quantities to the temperature required for setting. So now my kitchen counters are buried in jars of lumpy, bitter-sweet orange juice, the floor feels tacky underfoot and the whole lot will probably go mouldy as I forgot to get 'waxed disks', which Delia said were important. I have learnt to trust every word she says about the making of preserves.

This wasn't the most successful culinary endeavour if judged by edibility, but I am so glad we did it, and next year we'll do better, I'm sure. It would have made Mum so happy to see the three of us chatting away as we worked, digging up memories, sitting together in shared grief one minute, making each other snort with laughter the next. Even if it didn't have the right consistency, while it was cooking, our marmalade smelt the same as Mum's did. I would have done it for that alone.

The preparing, sharing and eating of food ties us across generations, cultures and miles. As with all God's good gifts it can be spoilt and corrupted – and it can be redeemed, making it again a sign of hope in the everlasting kingdom. I hope that one day you and I might feast around a table together, in this life or the one to come.

Go well, friend.

ACKNOWLEDGEMENTS

The first draft of this book came together in only three months, May, June and July of 2021. I was still somewhat shocked by Mum's absence, my brain taking time to rewire around the new reality, and being immersed in her writing was disorienting, both agonising and oddly comforting. It was an intense and challenging project, and I am grateful to my core that God blessed me with Andy Lyon as an editor. Andy, thank you for all you have poured into me and into *A Place at the Table*. You will always have a place at mine. Same goes for the whole Hodder Faith team. It is a great privilege to be part of the family.

Mum and I shared a love of beauty and the belief that aesthetics matter greatly. She would have had so much joy getting to know our designer, Karen Sawrey. Karen, kindred spirit and soul mate, thank you for making our book so gorgeous and for your loving, prayerful approach to each aspect of the design.

To 'the Originals' – Dad, Estie, Jem and Beth, thank you for trusting me with Mum's words. I know this has been an enormously painful process for you too. Thank you for all you have done to support and encourage me and for being some of my very favourite people in the world, as well as my family.

Thank you to all of my early readers, who each gave such thoughtful and observant feedback: Sharon Blair, Anita Cleverly (Mum's beloved sister), Mark and Rebecca Hannon and Carolyn Scriven.

Some of my friends put proper effort into carrying me while the book-making was in full swing. It took time, it took tissues, it took gin and tonic and prayer and patience, and they stuck at it. I don't take any of you for granted and I love you all very much: Thena, Abby, Lizzie, Ally, Alex, Ben, Laura, Bryony, Dan, Sarah Y and Sarah W, Júlio, Hedy and Pete, and Elaine.

Finally, to the three people with whom I spend most of my table-time: Shawn, Alexa and Charis, you are the best part of every day, even the really good ones.

Visit www.PlaceAtTheTable.info for photographs, recipes and more.

BOOK FOOD: AN ANNOTATED BIBLIOGRAPHY

BOOKS ABOUT FOOD AND DRINK

The Food we Eat
Joanna Blythman (London: Penguin, 1996)
I haven't read this, though Mum did several times and kept it in the kitchen for reference. I think I am still a little bitter about all the beans we ate because of what it said about meat production. It is the reason I will only buy free-range chicken, though, so it did its work.

The Forever Feast: Letting God Satisfy Your Deepest Hunger
Dr Paul Brand (Ann Arbor: Vine Books, 1993)
With insight on the body drawn from a long surgical career, Paul Brand explores what our appetites, dependence on food, digestive systems and more teach us about the genius of our Creator and the way he intended us to live in relationship with him and the world around us.

The Supper of the Lamb: A Culinary Reflection
Robert Farrar Capon (NY: Konecky & Konecky, 1967)
This is a quirky and intriguing meditation on cooking and, specifically, leg of lamb cooked four ways. I have Mum's copy given to her by Dad for Christmas 1996. He inscribed it, 'For Miranda, on the occasion of one of your own special feasts and in celebration of many to come, some theology for the preparations and some suggestions for the ministry.

'Appreciatively at your table, Peter.'

The Soul of Wine: Savoring the Goodness of God
Gisela H. Kreglinger (Downers Grove: IVP, 2019)
An invitation to discover how God's gift of wine can lead us into a more well-rounded, joy-filled, attentive spirituality. Gisela is the daughter of a vintner and a theologian. I am blessed to have experienced her wine-tastings and enjoyed her company around tables in Canada, Germany, Austria, France and England!

In Defense of Food: An Eater's Manifesto
Michael Pollan (New York: Penguin, 2008)
A compelling and, at times, rather nerve-wracking account of how food became over-complicated and often a bit nasty, and how we can find our way back to the basics of eating what tastes good and doesn't damage us or the planet.

RECIPE BOOKS
The Kitchen Revolution: A Year of Time and Money Saving Recipes
Rosie Sykes, Zoe Heron and Polly Russell (London: Ebury Press, 2007)
A few years ago, I was doing a book signing in a book shop. I sat at a table in a corner in front of the cookery book section and for two hours not a single customer gave me eye contact,

let alone a sale. I felt tears of shame building up and knew if I were to allow them to fall my public humiliation would be complete, so I pulled a random cookbook off the shelf and began to read. When it was time to pack up and leave, I bought *The Kitchen Revolution* and spent the next year cooking my way through it. The concept is brilliant: weekly meal plans that make the most of seasonally available ingredients, leftovers and preparation time. There are some meals to double so you can stock the freezer, some feasts and some simple weeknight suppers and, despite the odd memorably disgusting concoctions, family and friends all enjoyed this culinary adventure.

Salt, Fat, Acid, Heat: Mastering the Elements of Good Cooking
Samin Nosrat (Edinburgh: Canongate Books, 2017)
If you are someone who doesn't like to be constrained by recipes but find what you cook is more miss than hit when you freestyle it, this book is your new best friend. As well as containing recipes, it arms you with knowledge about the four main influencers of flavour so you can make good choices. Plus, it has gorgeous illustrations.

Jamie's Dinners
Jamie Oliver (London: Michael Joseph, 2004)
Almost every time someone is wildly complimentary about something I have cooked it is from a Jamie Oliver cookbook. He and I are very compatible chefs, by which I mean I prefer to chuck in herbs, lug the oil and measure by handful rather than by scales. I love how he puts food in the context of family and community life and cares about the earth and not just what it produces. If I ever got to meet him, I would melt into a star-struck puddle before I ever managed to tell him what an inspiration he has been to me, so I am telling him here. Jamie, you are the best.

Delia Smith's Complete Cookery Course
Delia Smith (London: Book Club Associates, 1983)
A real old friend, this brick-sized volume has travelled with me since I left home and has more food stains on its pages than any of my other cookbooks. There are no classic family favourites she doesn't cover, and if I actually obey her instructions, the result is always very pleasing.

BOOKS ABOUT HOSPITALITY AND COMMUNITY
Life Together
Dietrich Bonhoeffer (San Francisco: HarperCollins, 1954)
Drawn from what he learnt as part of an underground seminary in Nazi Germany, it is perhaps surprising how much of relevance there is for anyone living with other people anywhere, at any time in history. Looking at the role of prayer, work, worship and food, it provides a basis for a communal life where every member's faith is nurtured.

Daring Greatly: How the Courage to be Vulnerable Transforms the Way we Live, Love, Parent and Lead
Brené Brown (New York: Penguin, 2015)
The culmination of twelve years of social research, this is a call to be brave, to be seen and to take the risks that lead to the rewards of deep human connection. Brené Brown has been a pioneer in dismantling the stigma of vulnerability, showing it to be strength not weakness, and absolutely vital for anyone who wants to know and be known.

The Road to Daybreak: A Spiritual Journey
Henri Nouwen (London: Darton, Longman & Todd, 2013)
An intimate journal of a year spent living in a L'Arche community with adults with physical and learning difficulties, when Nouwen learnt more than ever before about God, himself and what it means to be human. This is a beautiful story told with

simplicity, humility and courage. One to read with tissues and a notebook on hand.

Making Room: Recovering Hospitality as a Christian Tradition
Christine D. Pohl (Grand Rapids: Eerdmans, 1999)
This is not a light read but it is worth the effort. I first read it when I was a student and have returned to it several times over the years when I have needed to come back to the heart of what hospitality as a Christian does and doesn't mean.

The Hidden Art of Homemaking: Creative Ideas for Enriching Everyday Life
Edith Schaeffer (London: The Norfolk Press, 1971)
Edith and her husband Francis founded the L'Abri movement by opening their Swiss home to young people in search of meaning, truth and belonging. A Rocha is among the many organisations inspired by their example of a community that embraces all and not just like-minded Christians. By all accounts, Edith was an Olympic standard home-maker. This book of hers inspired more than one generation to pay attention to the details, whether a centrepiece on the table, a jam jar of wild flowers on a window ledge or a candle softening the light of a bedroom in winter.

The Rituals of Dinner: The Origins, Evolution, Eccentricities and the Meaning of Table Manners
Margaret Visser (Toronto: HarperCollins, 1991)
A witty, wide-ranging and in-depth study on the history of how, when and where we eat. It made me realise how historically and culturally specific so much of the behaviour I might have considered normative actually is.

BOOKS ABOUT CREATION CARE
Planetwise: Dare to Care for God's World
Dave Bookless (London: IVP, 2008)
I first met Dave when I was thirteen and he still had hair! He has been living, studying and teaching about creation care for decades and he really knows his stuff. This book is a great place to start if you are just waking up to your environmental responsibility – it is practical, hopeful and totally non-judgemental.

Under the Bright Wings
Peter Harris (Vancouver: Regent College Publishing, 2000)
Written by my very own father, this is the story of the beginnings of A Rocha. Full of funny stories, improbably larger than life characters (including him!) and nail-biting hairpin bends in the road to becoming the worldwide phenomenon it is today. I promise you will love it, and not just because I'm his daughter.

Caring for Creation in Your Own Backyard
Loren and Mary Ruth Wilkinson (Vancouver: Regent College Publishing, 1996)
I had the very great privilege of studying under Loren and Mary Ruth at Regent College, courses like 'Books, Children and God' and 'The Christian Imagination', among others. I also spent time in their home on Galiano Island, feasting on home-made pasta, slabs of pacific salmon, vegetables and fruit from their plot of ocean-facing land. Every word they have written or spoken is worth its weight in gold, or, by a more appropriate measure, fertile soil.

NOTES

PROLOGUE

1 Leah Kostamo, *Planted: A Story of Creation, Calling, and Community* (Eugene: Wipf & Stock, 2013), p. 89.
2 Philip Yancey, *Prayer: Does it Make Any Difference?* (London: Hodder & Stoughton, 2006), p. 28.

1 HUNGER

1 For example, in a meta-analysis of twenty-nine long-term weight-loss studies, more than half of the lost weight was regained within two years, and by five years more than 80 per cent of lost weight was regained. J. W. Anderson, E. C. Konz, R. C. Frederich et al., 'Long-term weight-loss maintenance: a meta-analysis of US studies', *American Journal of Clinical Nutrition* 74 (5) (2001): 579–84.
2 Dr Paul Brand, *The Forever Feast: Letting God Satisfy Your Deepest Hunger* (Ann Arbor: Vine Books, 1993), pp. 23–4.
3 Sustainable Development Goal 2, Zero Hunger. United Nations Department of Economic and Social Affairs, sustainabledevelopment.un.org/sdg2 (accessed 10 February 2022).

4 Julianne Holt-Lunstad, Timothy B. Smith and J. Bradley Layton, 'Social Relationships and Mortality Risk: A Meta-Analytic Review', *PLOS Medicine 7*, no.7 (2010), https://doi.org/10.1371/journal.pmed.1000316 (accessed 10 February 2022); Julianne Holt-Lunstad, Timothy B. Smith, Mark Baker, Tyler Harris and David Stephenson, 'Loneliness and Social Isolation as Risk Factors for Mortality: A Meta-Analytic Review', *Perspectives on Psychological Science 10*, no.2 (2015): 227–37, https://doi.org/10.1177/1745691614568352 (accessed 10 February 2022); Amy Novotney, 'The Risks of Social Isolation', *Monitor on Psychology*, 50, no.5, (May 2019), www.apa.org/monitor/2019/05/ce-corner-isolation (accessed 10 February 2022). Cited Kate Murphy, *You're not Listening* (Dublin: Vintage, 2020, accessed online).

5 According to a 2017 government-commissioned report, 'Jo Cox Commission on Loneliness', Age UK, www.ageuk.org.uk/globalassets/age-uk/documents/reports-and-publications/reports-and-briefings/active-communities/rb_dec17_jocox_commission_finalreport.pdf (accessed 10 February 2022).

6 'Cigna U.S. Loneliness Index, 2018', Cigna, May 2018, www.multivu.com/players/English/8294451-cigna-us-loneliness-survey/docs/IndexReport_1524069371598-173525450.pdf (accessed 18 February 2022).

7 Henri Nouwen, *Life of the Beloved* (New York: Crossroad, 2002, accessed online).

8 Inspired by Matthew 14:13–21; Mark 6:31–44; Luke 9:12–17; John 6:1–13, 35, 53.

MIRANDA'S JOURNALS

1 ESV UK.

2 PREPARATION

1 Yancey, *Prayer*, p 33.

2 Joanna Blythman, *The Food We Eat: The Book You Cannot Afford to Ignore* (London: Penguin, 1996).

3 Inspired by Genesis 18:1–15.

3 WELCOME

1 Mary Douglas, 'Deciphering a meal', in *Implicit Meanings: Essays in Anthropology* (Oxford: Routledge, 1975) pp. 249–75.
2 1 Peter 4:7.
3 Inspired by Matthew 26:6–13; Mark 14:3–9; Luke 7:36–50; John 12:1–8.

MIRANDA'S JOURNALS

1 Romans 8:28 (NRSVA).

4 AT THE TABLE

1 The late John Stott was an early and significant pioneer of environmental theology and of A Rocha. As part of a series of articles Miranda wrote about his life on the A Rocha blog, she talked about how he embodied our organisational values of community and hospitality.
2 This insight came from Leon R. Kass, MD, *The Hungry Soul: Eating and the Perfecting of Our Nature* (London: The University of Chicago Press, 1994).
3 Dietrich Bonhoeffer, *Life Together* (San Francisco: HarperCollins, 1954), p. 68.
4 As told in the book by Isak Dinesen and the film based on the book, directed and written by Gabriel Axel.
5 Michael Pollan, *In Defense of Food: An Eater's Manifesto* (New York: Penguin, 2008).
6 Inspired by Matthew 26:17–30; Mark 14:12–26; Luke 22:7–39; John 13:1–17:26.

MIRANDA'S JOURNALS

1 The stable features in *The Last Battle* by C. S. Lewis, where it becomes a doorway between Narnia and the new Narnia.

5 THE CLEAN-UP

1 'Worldwide food waste', UN Environment Programme (undated), www.unep.org/thinkeatsave/get-informed/world-wide-food-waste (accessed 14 February 2022).

2 This story is told in Dave's book *Planetwise: Dare to Care for God's World* (Nottingham: IVP, 2008).

3 Liuan Huska and Ben Lowe, 'What Does Hope in Christ's Kingdom Have to Do with Climate Change?', *Christianity Today*, 15 July 2021, www.christianitytoday.com/better-samaritan/2021/july/what-does-hope-in-christs-kingdom-have-to-do-with-climate-c.html (accessed 14 February 2022).

4 Dostoevsky in Nicholas Berdyaev, *Dostoevsky* (New York: Living Age Books, 1957), p. 53, cited in Eugene H. Peterson, *Under the Unpredictable Plant: An Exploration in Vocational Holiness* (Grand Rapids: William B. Eerdmans, 1994), p. 58.

5 C. S. Lewis, *Surprised by Joy* (New York: Harcourt, Brace and World, 1955), pp. 226–9.

6 The actual wording of the quote is disputed, however. Jordan M. Poss, 'What's wrong, Chesterton?', 28 February 209, https://www.jordanmposs.com/blog/2019/2/27/whats-wrong-chesterton (accessed 18 February 2022).

7 Henri Nouwen, *Life of the Beloved* (accessed online).

8 'Presidential address to General Synod, By The Most Revd Rowan Williams, Archbishop of Canterbury', York, 14 July 2003, http://rowanwilliams.archbishopofcanterbury.org/articles.php/1826/archbishops-presidential-address-general-synod-york-july-2003.html (accessed 14 February 2022).

9 I have found Marshall B. Rosenberg, *Nonviolent Communication: A Language of Life,* third edition (Encinitas, CA: PuddleDancer Press, 2015) hugely enlightening on this.

10 Revelation 21:2.

11 Inspired by John 21:1–23.

MIRANDA'S JOURNALS

1 Romans 8:28.

6 THE FOREVER FEAST

1 Virginia Stem Owens, *And the Trees Clap their Hands: Faith, Perception and the New Physics* (Eugene: Wipf & Stock, 1983) p. 142.

2 Robert Farrar Capon, *The Supper of the Lamb: A Culinary Reflection* (New York: Konecky & Konecky, 1967), p. 189.

3 Eugene H. Peterson, *This Hallelujah Banquet: How the End of What We Were Reveals Who We Can Be* (Colorado Springs: Waterbrook, 2021), p. 153.

4 Inspired by John 11:1–44; 12:1–8.

MIRANDA'S JOURNALS

1 Vigen Guroian, *Life's Living towards Dying: A Theological and Medical-Ethical Study* (Grand Rapids: William B.Eerdmans, 1996), cited in John Wyatt, *Dying Well* (London: IVP, 2018, accessed online).

INTENSIVE CARE, SPOKEN TO VOICE MEMO

1 Christopher (Kit) Smart was an eighteenth-century poet known for his love of nature, who spent some time confined to St Luke's Hospital for Lunatics.

A ROCHA

Field notes podcast

We are living in a time of crisis for the planet. Our overuse and misuse of water, energy and food has led to dangerous levels of habitat loss, pollution, soil degradation and ocean acidification. As a result we face the giant issues of climate change, biodiversity loss, disease and poverty.

A Rocha has always been a voice of hope in the environmental space. *The Field notes podcast*, hosted by Peter Harris and Bryony Loveless, is an exploration of the ideas, practice and experience making a difference on the ground, through conversations with people who really know what they are talking about – from conservation scientists, explorers and biologists, to artists, entrepreneurs and theologians. They have hopeful stories to tell.

---

visit **arocha.org/podcast** for more info or listen via your favourite podcast app